PATRIOTISM
WITHOUT
FLAGS

Photo by Janis Leventhal

Daniel Lang is a member of the staff of *The New Yorker*, for which he served as war correspondent in Italy and France in World War II. He has written poetry and short stories. His books include *From Hiroshima to the Moon* and *Casualties of War*, a widely translated, prize-winning account of an American patrol in Vietnam.

Also by *Daniel Lang:*

EARLY TALES OF THE ATOMIC AGE
THE MAN IN THE THICK LEAD SUIT
FROM HIROSHIMA TO THE MOON
AN INQUIRY INTO ENOUGHNESS
CASUALTIES OF WAR

For children (fiction):
A SUMMER'S DUCKLING

LANG, Daniel. **Patriotism without flags.** Norton, 1974. 209p 74-
1360. 6.95.   ISBN 0-393-05521-3.   C.I.P.
Lang, a staff writer of *The New Yorker,* has here assembled six essays
(all of which appeared in slightly different form in *The New Yorker*
these past six years) dealing with various aspects of America's involvement with the war in Indo-China.   The book opens with Dr.
Spock's trial in 1968 in Boston.   The following chapter, "Out of it,"
shifts to a colony of American deserters in Sweden.   "Home again" is a
probing interview with a young ex-Marine who reflects upon his combat experience in Viet-Nam.   "AWOL" chronicles the life of a military
runaway.   "Love of country" recounts the experience of a Rochester
school-teacher who was dismissed for refusing to lead her class in reciting the Pledge of Allegiance.   A final chapter is entitled "The supreme option" and treats of the possibility of our having employed
the atom bomb in View-Nam.   The book's recurrent theme is that
patriotism is a highly individual matter.   "It is not enough to die for
one's country; one must also want to live in it," the author writes in
his foreword.   Beautifully written, here is a poignant, sometimes painful volume bearing a perfect title.

PATRIOTISM WITHOUT FLAGS

Daniel Lang

W · W · Norton & Company · Inc ·
New York

Copyright © 1974 by Daniel Lang
First Edition

Library of Congress Cataloging in Publication Data

Lang, Daniel.
Patriotism without flags.

1. Vietnamese Conflict, 1961–   —United States—
Addresses, essays, lectures. 2. Patriotism—United
States—Addresses, essays, lectures. I. Title.
DS557.A63L36   1974   959.704'33'73   74–1360
ISBN 0–393–05521–3

Published simultaneously in Canada
by George J. McLeod Limited, Toronto

With the exception of the Foreword, the contents of this book
appeared in *The New Yorker* in slightly different form.
Charles Patrick Crow gave me valuable help in the
preparation of this book, for which he has my gratitude.

*This book was designed by Margaret F. Plympton.
Typefaces used are Caledonia and Craw Modern,
set by Unitron Graphics, Inc.
Printing and binding were done by Vail-Ballou Press, Inc.*

Printed in the United States of America

1 2 3 4 5 6 7 8 9 0

To M. L., Encore

CONTENTS

—But do you know what a nation means? says John Wyse.

—Yes, says Bloom.

—What is it? says John Wyse.

—A nation? says Bloom. A nation is the same people living in the same place.

—By God, then, says Ned, laughing, if that's so I'm a nation for I'm living in the same place for the past five years.

So of course everyone had a laugh at Bloom and says he, trying to muck out of it:

—Or also living in different places.

—James Joyce, *Ulysses*

FOREWORD

In my view, America's military performance in Southeast Asia has brought patriotism to trial. Nor is this effect confined to America's borders. The fighting in Indo-China, I believe, has left nationals everywhere pondering the meaning of their country to themselves, for, with each foray that American administrations sponsored on that distant battlefield, citizens in all lands became increasingly conscious of the nature of national sovereignty. Each carpet-bombing run, each search-and-destroy mission, it appears to me, disseminated the message that nations are essentially mechanisms for the practice of large-scale violence. Each day the war lasted, its broad outline took on the intelligibility of a diagram. Given a strong power, the diagram said, that wants something of a weak one (military bases, oil, or whatever), what happens if the two reach no paper accord? Answer: Big Boy weighs in with his superior equipment and troops and helps himself to his prize. Naturally, he avoids conflict with military peers; such conflict would only turn a sure thing into a gamble. As we know, this scenario didn't come to pass, but it was its mentality, on display for a decade, that formed the popular impression of the Vietnam war. Daily, in homes throughout the world, individuals could literally bear witness to the sight of a superpower beating

up on an agricultural country, and what they saw, I
submit, exposed the workings of national sovereignties as
no other war has ever done.

This may seem a narrow, jaundiced picture to those
who look upon nations as comprising something better
than a merciless pecking order. Think of the heroes who
have died for their country, they may protest; think of the
poets who have sung its glories. All I can reply is that the
heroes and the poets, as well as lesser mortals, were
individuals, not governments, and that if the Vietnam war
demonstrated anything, it was that individuals and
governments are quite distinct propositions. This is as
true for small countries as it is for superpowers, but the
point, I think, takes on more meaning when applied to the
superpowers. If it is used in relation to North Vietnam, to
stick to the example at hand, one finds, looking back, that,
apart from surrendering, America's foe could not have
done other than what it did. Attacked by a mighty
foreigner, its inhabitants and their leaders fought for their
lives—a joint, desperate goal that allowed no significant
gap to divide people and government. But it was the
opposite that held for America. In no danger, it had no
clear-cut cause with which to fire its population. As a
result, the longer the war went on, the wider the gap grew
between Washington and its constituency; indeed, in
retrospect, the wonder of it all is not that the United
States failed of conquest but that it fared as well as it did.

Individual Americans had no recourse but to make of
the war what they would, the government's policy, if that
is the word, apparently consisting of an unwillingness to
win, lose, or draw. A thousand opinions arose, each at
variance with the other, all splintering the ranks of both
the hawks and the doves. An extremist wing of hawks, for
example, would have employed nuclear weapons to attain
victory. Few Americans gave voice to this idea, but,
nevertheless, I believe, it was one that lurked darkly in
many people's minds; in fact, I would say that the
possibility of nuclear hostilities not only hovered over the

Vietnam war (Chapter Four) but that it now necessarily frames all wars, of whatever size, investing them with stakes of unseemly dimension. As for the doves, their camp numbered those who would impeach Presidents or refuse to pay taxes or, for sure, have America withdraw unilaterally from Indo-China (Chapter One). Most Americans, though, casting about for leadership, turned to their government in a spirit of conditioned trust. For their trouble, they made the appalling discovery that their government, its course ever vague, could be more form than substance in time of war. Abandoned to themselves in this fashion, those legions of faithful, in seeking answers, could only ask themselves questions, quietly, discreetly, reluctantly. How may one be patriotic without guidance from one's government? What is patriotism, anyway? Is this war worth my son's life? Is it possible that my government has made an error? If it has, would it confess to it? Would other countries? Could a war like this one happen again? Devout citizens do not easily come by such questions, but once the questions are raised, I believe, answers will be forthcoming. What they will be and how they will eventually assert themselves are mysteries at this point, but it is my belief that their impact, when it is felt, will make it harder than ever for governments, including dictatorships, to lead their citizens into war.

These thoughts have occurred to me while going over the galleys of this book. It wasn't written with any thesis in mind, but, I now observe, nearly everyone in it is concerned with trying to figure out what he thinks of his country, whether he is Dr. Spock or the barely literate deserter in Sweden who assured me that America would be just great if only "a few things [were] changed there, like foreign policy and race." In short, these various individuals wish to be patriotic but without forfeiting the aspirations within themselves that would make their patriotism worth anything. It took the war in Vietnam to interest them in their sense of patriotism, and the reason for that, in my opinion, is that this time, in contrast to its prosecution of other wars, the government overreached itself. It pulled rank on its citizenry, ordering it into battle, asking sacrifices for inchoate, willful reasons. There were bound to be reactions—not that they ever assumed ideological shape. Rather, their underlying character was, as I have mentioned, of a surprised, inquisitive sort. If there is anything good to be said for the war, it is that it succeeded in arousing in many Americans, both hawks and doves, a long dormant awareness of their individuality. Without that, it seems to me, they could never have become curious about the origins of their patriotism, for it takes a certain irreverence to contemplate one's country in terms of one's own vision of it. I think that the war blurred that vision for most Americans and that their patriotic instincts have been dulled. I regret this, for, as expatriates have often attested, patriotism is a part of our makeup; it contributes to our sense of identity; it gives us a place to love. As the war has shown, however, national sovereignties grow less lovable, their readiness to issue marching orders and to wave flags steadily more pronounced. Perhaps nations will have to be supplanted as objects of patriotism—they are not verities; there was a time, centuries ago, when they were unknown. But if nations are here to stay, then their managers will do well to remember that each of their subjects carries a private vision of his country's value; the more this is discounted, the more scrutiny will the managers attract. It is not enough to die for one's country; one must also want to live in it.

PATRIOTISM WITHOUT FLAGS

1

THE TRIAL OF DR. SPOCK

ヒ ヒ ヒ ヒ ヒ

A week or so before the conspiracy trial of Dr. Benjamin Spock and four other opponents of the Vietnam war opened in Boston on May 20, 1968, the sitting judge, Francis J. W. Ford, discussing ground rules in his chambers with government and defense counsel, stipulated that one of the defendants, the Reverend Dr. William Sloane Coffin, Jr., who was the chaplain of Yale University, was to be addressed in court not by his ecclesiastical title but as Defendant Coffin. Judge Ford, an imperious man of eighty-five who early in the proceedings characterized himself as "a slave to regularity," gave no reason for the legalistic unfrocking, but his intent may have been to draw a sharp line of demarcation between considerations of law and those of conscience and belief. This was certainly on his mind throughout the trial itself, for time and again spectators in his courtroom—a small one in the Federal Building— heard him instruct counsel and the jury to guard against the intrusion of extraneous matters and confine their

thinking to the letter of the indictment at hand. As the
sessions approached their end, after nearly four weeks, it
was dazzlingly clear that the elderly magistrate, his
hearing strained and his demeanor cantankerous, had set
himself a difficult course. The case was simply too
palpably entwined with controversial public issues
—with the question of dove versus hawk—for its legal
form and its social content to be separable. The terms
"conscience" and "belief" became stale with use, so often
were they uttered, not only by the defense but by the
government itself—the author of the indictment that
Judge Ford strove so valiantly to keep ever paramount in
the minds of all. In fact, it was the government
prosecutor—John Wall, a thirty-six-year-old former paratrooper in Korea—who took the initiative in this. He had
little choice. Nearly all his evidence was based on public
appearances of the alleged conspirators in which (as Wall
presented it in court) one defendant or another gave it as
his "belief" that the exercise of "conscience" could
deflect America from pursuing an "immoral"—as well as
an "unconstitutional" and "illegal"—war in Vietnam. To
dramatize this evidence, the courtroom was darkened
over a period of days while television-news clips,
projected on a large screen facing the jury, showed the
various defendants holding forth—at an outdoor rally, at
a press conference, at a church service in Boston at which
young men filed past a flaming taper and some of them
incinerated their draft cards. By the time the lawyers
offered their summations, things had loosened up to the
point where the 1968 Presidential race was being
weighed. This occurred when Wall, stoutly denying that
the government was conducting a political trial, scoffed at
the notion that war protesters like the defendants could
have influenced President Johnson's decision to quit the
White House. "If Johnson did retire involuntarily," he
told the jury, "I submit to you the reason he did, if he did,
was because a man named Eugene McCarthy and a man

named Robert Kennedy . . . through the regular political process—the ballot box—brought it about."

The case before Judge Ford might not have wandered as far afield as it did—or, at least, might not have done so as often—if it had not been for the catchall nature of the government's indictment. It charged conspiracy, stating that the aims of the plot had been to "counsel, aid, and abet" draftable men to avoid military service and dispense with carrying draft cards and classification notices, and to "hinder and interfere with" the administration of the Military Selective Service Act of 1967. However, it was not these aims that were at issue but, rather, the government's claim that the defendants had formed a conspiracy to achieve them; in short, it wasn't *what* the five men had done but that they had got together to do it. Unfortunately, the distinction was not always readily apparent. It was sometimes lost even on Wall himself. In ticking off the aims of the conspiracy for the jury at the outset of the trial, he said that the government charged the defendants with those aims. Chaplain Coffin's attorney objected, and Wall quickly corrected himself, saying that the indictment "doesn't charge the substantive offenses" but "charges the defendants with conspiring to commit these acts," and adding that "certainly the objection of counsel is well taken."

"Members of the jury," Judge Ford put in at this point, "a conspiracy may be defined as a breathing together, a plan, an agreeing together."

Known in legal circles, because of its latitude, as "the prosecutor's delight," the conspiracy charge is generally employed against gangsters—as it was, notably, in 1959, when twenty-seven Mafia leaders were brought to book for having breathed together in the upstate New York village of Apalachin. However, when it is applied to cases involving dissent, such as the Spock case, the latitude that delights a prosecutor may also raise the question of whether freedom of speech and of assembly and the other

civil liberties guaranteed by the First Amendment are
being abrogated. Reflecting this latitude, the indictment
not only charged the five defendants in Judge Ford's
courtroom with conspiracy but accused "divers other
persons, some known and others unknown," as "co-conspirators." Frequently, individuals were named in the
testimony who *sounded* as though they might have been
co-conspirators, their anti-draft activity being described
in such detail that one was left puzzled over why they,
too, weren't defendants. Speaking of one of these
non-defendants (a linguistics professor at M.I.T.), Wall
said, "At least he is not sitting at the bar as a defendant
today," underscoring the word so portentously that he
drew a laugh from the spectators.

The indictment's epidemic potentialities were brought
out when the government offered in evidence an anti-war
manifesto entitled "A Call to Resist Illegitimate Authority," and its signers, who numbered some thirty-five
hundred, were implicated as possible co-conspirators.
Before the trial was over, the question arose of whether
Mayor   Lindsay   had   behaved   co-conspiratorially
when—as he revealed at the trial, testifying for Dr.
Spock—he had collaborated with the organizers of a
sitdown demonstration at the Whitehall Street induction
center by helping to formulate the arrangements for it,
right down to the manner in which arrests were to be
made. When Dr. Spock's attorney, Leonard B. Boudin,
inquired who the "divers other persons" of the indictment might be, Wall referred him to the television-news
clips, inviting him to look at the faces of the persons
attending the rallies. Judge Ford appeared to lend
sanction to the prosecutor's position by instructing the
jury that if any of the five defendants were to be found
guilty, their public statements would be "chargeable and
admissible as to all others you likewise find to be
members of the conspiracy, whether or not the person . . . is named in the indictment."

A theory put forward by visiting lawyers had it that the

Boston Five, as many newspapers called the defendants, owed their indictment to the fortuitous circumstance that their anti-draft activities had been abundantly recorded in publications and on television. According to the theory, this made the men's prosecution attractive as a practical proposition, for the publicity provided the government with a rich supply of evidence deemed usable. Criminal conspiracy, the law states, need not be conducted in secrecy—even though the charge is generally directed against embezzlers, extortionists, and other types of clandestine operators. At no point in the proceedings was evidence adduced to show that there had been undercover meetings, correspondence, or telephone calls. Television appearances, radio interviews, published articles, press conferences, petitions to the United States Attorney General, mass meetings in New York, Washington, and Boston—these constituted the evidence cited by the government as proof of a functioning conspiracy. The defense attorneys denied that the evidence proved any such thing , maintaining that it proved only that the accused were trying to reach as many millions of people as possible with their anti-war message. What self-respecting conspirators, they asked, would trumpet their plot for all to hear? Boudin sardonically labelled it "the mass-media conspiracy," but neither he nor his colleagues ever argued that secrecy was a precondition of illegal conspiracy.

Another aspect of the latitude afforded by "the prosecutor's delight" is that there is no need to prove that the alleged conspirators know each other—fortunately for the government, in this case, since testimony brought out that the five accused had never been together privately until after their indictment, in January of that year, when they and their counsel had gathered in Boudin's apartment in New York. Prior to that, their contact with each other had been sketchy and public. Dr. Spock, for example, had been introduced to Chaplain Coffin on the platform at a Madison Square Garden rally. Michael

Ferber, a twenty-three-year-old graduate student at
Harvard, had met Chaplain Coffin when the two officiated
at a service held in a Boston church, and Mitchell
Goodman, a forty-four-year-old teacher and writer, and
Marcus Raskin, thirty-three years old and the director of
the Institute of Policy Studies, a non-profit educational
institution in Washington, had had similarly superficial
encounters. Upon inquiring why it wasn't necessary for
conspirators to be acquainted, I received an answer from
John K. Van de Kamp, a Department of Justice lawyer,
who was the director of a newly established unit for
prosecuting Selective Service cases, and who had come
up from the capital for the trial. Relying on analogy and
metaphor, Van de Kamp told me, "Suppose there's a big
shipment of narcotics smuggled into the country from
Sicily. Well, it might be sold to one man, who then
divides it and sells it to several other individuals, who
then do the same thing, until the stuff is in the hands of
any number of small-time pushers. You'd hardly expect
all these people to know each other, but, just the same,
they would be partners in a conspiracy." Two days later,
in court, Wall gave an illustration of conspiracy, which
impressed Van de Kamp, and he advised me to study it.
The illustration was based on a movie called "The
Killing," in which the central character recruits a wide
variety of accomplices in order to rob a race track. The
shady roster, Wall informed the court, includes a
race-track bartender, who on the day of the robbery is to
get into a fight with a chess player, a second hireling.
Another man, posing as a disabled veteran, is supposed to
shoot a race horse, "to cause great confusion at the same
time that the fight started to distract the police." Then,
there is a teller, whose contribution is to agree to let "the
main perpetrator of the conspiracy" make off with the
money in the teller's care, after which enter two new
characters—a payoff man and a crooked cop acting as
bagman for the outfit's mastermind. The next time I saw
Van de Kamp, I asked who the main perpetrator in the

Spock case was. He shook his head and said, "That wasn't the point of the illustration."

Even the selecting of jurors was marked by a certain latitude. When the jury was finally chosen, it was made up, in the old phrase, of twelve good men and true, for the government would have no women, peremptorily challenging those whose names had been drawn. The general conjecture was that the prosecution thought women might have strong misgivings about the violence taking place in Vietnam, or else might remember midnights when Dr. Spock's famous book on child care had enabled them to relieve a croupy infant. Whatever its reasons, the government didn't have many women to challenge. Of a total of eighty-eight veniremen summoned, only nine were women, and Boudin, arguing that this did not represent a fair cross-section of the community, called on the court clerk, Russell H. Peck, for an explanation. "It makes me look like a misogynist," Peck said, on the witness stand. He was asked whether he followed any particular method in choosing veniremen from police lists, and he replied, "I put my finger on the place and on a name and then I make a mark next to it with a pen."

Q.: "Do you do that by not looking at the page?"

A.: "I have to look at it enough to know where it is in relation to my finger. . . . I do not intend to look carefully at the name. Actually, this is not a job that is terribly inspiring. After one has done it a few times, there isn't much joy in reading the name."

There was one college graduate on the jury—an architect. Four other jurymen had had some college education, and five more had completed high school. The twelve included a meat cutter, a loan supervisor at a bank, a customer-service man with Eastern Airlines, an engineer, a "self-employed" man, two printers, two electronics technicians, a construction foreman, and a hardware clerk. Their average age was thirty-eight, and all of them were white, the government having challenged the one Negro whose name had been drawn.

The longer the trial went on, the more discernibly it seemed to develop a life and character of its own. Daily, the small courtroom was filled to capacity, its doors shutting out an overflow of spectators. Many of those who got in, as well as those who tried to, wore peace buttons, but opponents of their position also appeared. One day, a soldier home from Vietnam, his left hand in a splint, joined the line of would-be spectators, and upon being interviewed by a local reporter he attacked those who shared the defendants' attitude toward the war. On another occasion, a contingent of thirty Wellesley girls in caps and gowns turned up in the marble corridor outside the courtroom to tell Chaplain Coffin they were sorry that he hadn't been able to deliver the baccalaureate address at their graduation ceremonies, as he had been invited to do. Whenever Judge Ford declared a brief recess, a promenade of spectators, press representatives, lawyers, and defendants ensued outside, and the corridor echoed with their talk, which often had to do with the possible significance of this or that bit of testimony, or with whether this or that juror had the look of a dove or a hawk. The defendants joined in the speculation—they were always approachable, appearing as willing to talk with strangers as with friends and relatives. Sometimes the speculation had to do with the impression that well-known witnesses had made while they were testifying, since there were many of these, among them—in addition to Mayor Lindsay—United States Senator Stephen M. Young, of Ohio; Congressman William F. Ryan, of New York; and Dr. Jerome B. Wiesner, former science adviser to Presidents Kennedy and Johnson and later president of M.I.T. Wall and his staff vanished from view during these intermissions, descending into the United States Attorney's offices, on the floor below. The defense lawyers were around, however, listening—sometimes with a look of omniscience—to suggestions from well-wishers. Occasionally, pacing the corridor with one or another of the lawyers, I would hear my companion complain about the forensic preenings of some colleague, for the defenders of the defendants were far from constituting a coordinated team. More than once, before Judge Ford's bench, they objected to each other's argument.

Inside the courtroom, all was punctilio, beginning with the court crier's archaic greeting of "Hear ye! Hear ye!" each morning. Like burly movie ushers, marshals roamed the aisles during the trial. The defendants' families, occupying two reserved rows, formed a special community. The defendants themselves sat together in chairs up front, separated from the spectators by a brass railing. The lawyers were restless onstage, arguing and holding whispered conferences as, in varying degrees, each went about trying to remake his client in his own image. In the jury box, the twelve men sat expressionless throughout, their attention apparently unflagging. (Late in the trial, though, one of them did doze off awhile.) And, finally, enthroned on his high bench, his robes enfolding his portly figure, Judge Ford gazed out over his domain.

Recurring week after week, this fixed, formalized scene achieved a certain solemnity, yet at times it was difficult to bear in mind that the proceedings could result in five years' imprisonment and a ten-thousand-dollar fine for each defendant. Perhaps this difficulty derived from the fact that the defendants were not accused of "substantive offenses," for this tended to make the government look as though it were casting aspersions rather than charging a crime. Nor did the reliance on evidence that had long been publicly known do anything to mitigate that impression. Among the prosecution witnesses, for example, were a number of television cameramen who, having unwittingly served a federal sponsor, were called to identify themselves as the men who had filmed the clips being shown the jury. Even when the government produced an undercover agent who had been assigned to turn up evidence, his information consisted of a report on a publicized event. Special Agent Lawrence E. Miller, of the Federal Bureau of Investigation, upon being called to the witness stand, testified that he had done his sleuthing at a press conference held in October, 1967, at the New York Hilton Hotel—a conference that his superiors had learned about from reading the New York *Daily News*. At this press conference, four of the five men destined to be indicted were airing their anti-war views, as were other individuals. Miller testified that, concealing his identity, he joined dozens of reporters and cameramen, helped himself to handouts, and then, like the reporters, took out a notebook and made entries in it. Miller's journalistic adventure met with rough handling in court. Among the facts that the defense lawyers extracted from Miller was that he had never before been assigned to cover a conference concerned with public affairs, and that his notes did not represent the content of the conference "either in substance or . . . gist." The notes did tell of plans for anti-war demonstrations in different parts of the country, but as Miller granted, these plans were already public knowledge. Miller's notes also appeared to be at variance with the F.B.I.'s long-standing contention that it sticks to the gathering of "raw material," leaving the "evaluation" of the material to others. As became clear from Miller's testimony, he was stirred to instant evaluation on hearing Raskin deny at the conference that the President necessarily knew more about the Vietnamese situation than other Americans did. "Baloney," Miller wrote in his reporter's book—though he discreetly enclosed the word in parentheses.

Another factor that detracted from the unquestionable seriousness of the proceedings was the general inefficiency of the alleged conspiracy—at least, as it was revealed in court. United though the defendants were in opposing the war, each seemed to emphasize a different incentive for pressing his opposition. Dr. Spock, it was brought out, was exercised by a belief that the war was sullying the good name of the United States at home and abroad by killing its own and foreign youth and by diverting funds that might be better spent on the impoverished. Raskin was preoccupied with advocating the setting up of a commission to investigate the legality of the war. Goodman was intent on obtaining the support of older people for those resisting conscription. Chaplain Coffin wanted the Selective Service Act overhauled to legitimize the status both of non-believer objectors and of selective conscientious objectors, who hold that an individual may object to a particular war but not necessarily to all wars. And the overriding interest of Ferber, the youngest of the defendants, was in building a "community" of his contemporaries to stand fast in resisting the draft in such great numbers that the government would have to reconsider its present course. Ferber, who was born a Unitarian and opposed the draft on religious rather than political grounds, had turned in his card seven months earlier.

Needless to say, the degree of the defendants' efficiency as alleged conspirators had no bearing on their guilt or innocence. Nevertheless, it was not difficult to find detached spectators who believed that the government was insufficiently threatened to warrant its going to so much judicial trouble. (One such spectator remarked, "The government has bitten off less than it can chew.") The following interchange between Wall and Raskin gave scant indication that the republic was imperilled:

Q.: "And you heard the speeches that were made there [at the press conference] that day?"

A.: "I heard, yes."

Q.: "And you heard— Pardon me?"

A.: "I heard but didn't listen."

Q.: "Well, why didn't you listen?"

A.: "They were boring."

Nor was Goodman's account of the sitdown at the Whitehall Street induction center easily construed as a show of conspiratorial mettle. In accordance with the plan agreed to by Mayor Lindsay, the demonstrators eventually did invite arrest by sitting on the steps of the induction center for two or three minutes, but only after a jumble of incidents had appeared to jeopardize the arrangement. Here we have Goodman pondering—in response to questions put by his attorneys—the problem of what to do until the paddy wagon comes. It was the early morning of December 5, 1967, and he had just arrived by subway to take part in the demonstration, which was organized by the War Resisters League, a pacifist organization, of which David McReynolds is field secretary.

Q.: "What time was it, about?"

A.: "I must have gotten there about quarter of six. . . . It was dark and somewhat confusing and I didn't know where I was. People were milling around. Everyone seemed to be looking for . . . someone to tell them what to do. I noticed there were a great many police. Then someone indicated to me that there was a platform and a man standing on it with a microphone. . . ."

Q.: "How far was that from the induction center?"

A.: "That was about two blocks from the front of the Whitehall Street building. . . . I moved over toward the platform, where I met a number of people I knew in New York who were down there as well, and then I realize it was David McReynolds on the platform and I knew that he was the organizer."

Q.: "Did he give some directions or something at that point?"

A.: "Yes. . . . After a few minutes, he said, 'Those who want to commit civil disobedience form on this side and those who want simply to be in a legal picket line form on that side.' I moved over to the right side; I knew I was going to be in the civil-disobedience part of it. We got together in a very rough formation and I found Dr. Spock there. . . . I was pleased and surprised to see him. . . ."

Q.: "How far were you from the induction center at this point?"

A.: "We [were] still about two blocks away. . . . There was this fairly large group of people moving along, and they were being pushed right and left by news

photographers and television men who were creating a
terrible scramble. It was hard to keep organized. We went
around the corner, and [there] was a police bar-
ricade . . . and a lot of policemen. They stopped us. And
one of us explained that we . . . had made prearrange-
ments to come to . . . this civil-disobedience thing. . . .
They opened the barrier and let us through. It was so dark
and so confused I can't say how many people were in the
group—maybe twenty or thirty."

Q.: "About how far were you from the induction center
at that time?"

A.: "We were about a block away. . . . We moved over
toward the barrier directly in front of the entrance of the
building, which we knew was where we ought to be. . . .
There was a large number of police officers massed on the
steps of the building. . . . My assumption, my thought,
was that we would be allowed to enter there. . . ."

Q.: "What happened there?"

A.: "Nothing seemed to happen. We just stood there."

Q.: "Who is 'we' at this point?"

A.: "I was standing next to Dr. Spock, and Dr. Spock
was so thoroughly surrounded by newspapermen and
television people we were isolated from everybody else."

Q.: "What happened at that point?"

A.: "We stood there for a few moments and Dr. Spock
said to me, 'What are we supposed to do?' And I said to
him, 'Well, I don't really know, but we are supposed to
get through here to that place on the sidewalk. The only
one who really knows is David McReynolds.' At that
point . . . I shouted to some people behind us, 'Where's
David McReynolds?' Nobody knew. And so Dr. Spock
. . . said to me, 'Well, we can't just stand here. This is
foolish.' And so the next thing he did was to get down on
his hands and knees to try to get under the barrier."

Q.: "And did you?"

A.: "I got under there with him—right."

Q.: "What happened then? . . ."

A.: "We stayed there, thinking the police would let us

through for a few moments, and they didn't. . . . I started
to call for Inspector Garelik, the Chief Inspector of the
New York City police force. . . ."

Q.: "Then what happened?"

A.: "There was no response, and Dr. Spock said again,
'Well, this is foolish, just standing here. I thought that
arrangements had been made for us to go through. . . .'"

Q.: "After you and Dr. Spock were still figuring out
what to do, what then happened?"

A.: "Dr. Spock put his leg up on the barrier and tried to
get up on it and the police officers behind the barrier put
their arms up. They were obviously intent on not hurting
him. . . . Some poeple behind him put their arms up and
held him there."

Q.: "He was caught in between?"

A.: "Yes."

Q.: "What did you do?"

A.: "I just stood there. . . . Then I called for Inspector
Garelik."

Inside the courtroom, there were no echoes of the
impromptu heroics of the street. Only decorum reigned,
the rules and maneuverings of judicial procedure—rea-
sonable, coded, prissy, and as intricate as those of an
adult game, which the initiated alone could play. Like
doting relatives, the defense attorneys had their wards
display their merit badges. Goodman, the spectators
learned, had been an artilleryman in the Second World
War, and Dr. Spock had been a naval officer (and he had
supported NATO and the Korean war), and Chaplain
Coffin not only had served splendidly in the Second
World War but had also been a C.I.A. agent for three years
during the Korean war, entrusted with top secrets he
couldn't talk about to this day. In the corridor during
recesses, young spectators wearing peace buttons expressed chagrin at the unhortatory nature of the proceedings, but none of these young people, I thought, sounded
as deeply thwarted as Chaplain Coffin did in a conversa-

tion I had with him during one court break. On the stand,
the Chaplain was hardly the picture of a clerical crusader.
A practiced speaker, he sometimes seemed a little too
practiced, easily coping with Wall's questions while
keeping his eyes on the jury. An erudite man (he could
have testified in French, German, or Russian), he made
references at one point or another to St. Peter, Socrates,
and Péguy, but the blank gaze of his peers in the jury box
turned his words into hollow name-dropping. As it
happened, Chaplain Coffin had campaigned more persist-
ently than any of the other defendants for a trial
concerning the anti-war protests, for he had a strong
confidence in the courts, born of his experiences as a
Freedom Rider in Alabama several years earlier, when he
and others had violated a local law segregating bus
passengers; a test case had followed, and the Supreme
Court had overthrown the statute. In Boston, Wall
reminded Chaplain Coffin of his long campaign for a
legal confrontation on Vietnam. The gambit left the
impression that the Chaplain had only himself to blame
for being in the dock, but in fact Chaplain Coffin hadn't
got the trial he was seeking. "I wanted a trial of stature,"
he told me during a recess. "I wanted to test the legality of
the war and the constitutionality of the Selective Service
Act. I wanted a trial that might be of help to selective
conscientious objectors. But this—what is it?" I asked
whether he thought one had to undergo punishment to
demonstrate the sincerity of one's beliefs. "You're
speaking of martyrdom, aren't you?" he replied, smiling
remotely. " 'Martyr' is a Greek word, you know—it means
'witness.' I must do whatever is necessary to bear witness,
but why should that mean I must count on suffering for
doing what I believe to be right?"

Unlike Chaplain Coffin, Ferber had set no particular
store by a legal confrontation. As a bachelor of
twenty-three, he lived on close terms with the war, and
could speak about it naturally, almost occupationally.
Ferber, a thin, neat, seemingly lighthearted English-liter-

ature scholar who had graduated *summa cum laude* from
Swarthmore in 1966 and won a Woodrow Wilson
fellowship to Harvard, told me over lunch one day that
although he had a decent regard for the judicial process,
he wondered whether the trial had any relevance to the
peace movement. "That's going to go on, regardless of
what happens to us," he said. "Last year, hundreds of my
contemporaries were put in prison for resisting the draft,
and that hasn't stopped the movement." He regretted that
Judge Ford had forbidden the defendants to invoke the
Nuremberg principles, which make individual citizens
responsible for the conduct of their government; exclud-
ing the Nuremberg principles, Ferber said, was tantamount to holding Eichmann up as an example of a
law-abiding burgher. Still, Ferber thought the trial had its
points. Since he and the others had been indicted, he said,
great numbers of Americans had joined the anti-draft
ranks. "Spock's flock is rocking," he went on, reciting a
post-indictment slogan. "The trial has conferred a
legitimacy on the movement. Tell me, you don't think
we've become a part of the Establishment, do you?"

It became increasingly plain as the trial progressed that
it wasn't going to shed any light on the issue of the legal
limits of dissent, which, in the opinion of both the doves
and the hawks among the spectators, was probably the
most valuable contribution that the proceedings might
have made, for until this issue was clarified the country
would remain perplexed about where individual conscience leaves off and national needs take over. Sweeping
matters of this sort, however, were far from the
government's conception of the case, since it leaned so
strongly in the direction of form rather than substance.
The government lawyers I talked with said they saw
nothing wrong with the case, but it was possible to detect
signs that they were not impervious to the doubts of
others. One of them told me one day that his mother had
sent him a clipping from a British weekly in which a
correspondent had described the trial as a replay of the

McCarthyism of the nineteen-fifties. "I don't believe that," the government man said emphatically. Another day, an important member of the prosecution team remarked during a visit I paid him in his office, "We know these five men aren't ordinary criminals in mentality. But that's the tragedy of it. Why couldn't they have protested by using their vote, the way most people do?" Tragedy or not, the government had prepared its case thoroughly. Van de Kamp, who was in his thirties and was unmarried, told me that he had even read Dr. Spock's book on infant care from cover to cover, and that it had recently enabled him to advise a secretary in his office how to treat her baby's colic.

Almost from the outset, everyone I met assumed that bad news lay ahead for the defendants—for all of them except Raskin, that is, who, as the testimony unfolded, was given a chance of acquittal. The evidence adduced in Boston showed that he had never challenged the government to a legal confrontation or taken part in a sitdown, and that he regarded the turning in of draft cards as "silly", his advocacy of a commission to look into the legality of the war was barely controversial; and also going for him was the fact that several witnesses cast considerable doubt on the government's identification of him as a vociferous protester who had demanded that a Department of Justice official accept a briefcase filled with turned-in draft cards. There were a number of reasons for the poor prognosis for the other defendants. One was a general belief that there must be something to the charge, since the government had staked its authority on the outcome of the case. Another was the latitude of the charge, combined with the difficulty of keeping it separate from "substantive offenses." It was also conjectured that the jurors might feel they were endorsing civil disobedience if they returned a verdict of not guilty. A Harvard chemist who attended a few sessions observed to me, "The defendants are raising difficult questions, for which they have no clear-cut answers. They're asking the

country to give up old ways for unfamiliar ones." Finally,
the defendants had to contend with Judge Ford's
management of the trial, which, unfortunately, was not
always evenhanded.

The official transcript—nineteen mimeographed volumes—includes examples of Judge Ford's style, but its
inanimate contents, in the words of the Washington
Post's judicial correspondent, "do not convey the manner
in which 85-year-old Judge Francis J. W. Ford showed
his disbelief in the defense case and his tolerance for the
Government's." (The same correspondent, John P.
MacKenzie, wrote, "The Judge's display of bias . . . deprived the Nation of a trial that was fundamentally fair.")
The official transcript does not convey the skeptical tone
that the Judge employed in addressing defendants when
they denied government allegations. Nor does anything
in its nineteen volumes describe his elaborate shuffling of
papers and ordering about of clerks and marshals when
defense attorneys were scoring points—though the
transcript does show that he sometimes capped such
points by admonishing the jury to keep an open mind. In
reading the transcript, one cannot hear his hectoring tone
as he urged defense lawyers to "get on" or "go forward"
on numerous occasions—something he rarely did to the
prosecution. When a defense lawyer elicited testimony
from Dr. Spock that many Americans agreed with him,
the Judge said, "Strike it out." The lawyer then asked
whether Dr. Spock had met persons who disagreed with
him, and Dr. Spock said, "Yes." "Let it stand," the Judge
said. " . . . It is obvious. . . . The Court can take
judicial notice of that." Upon becoming irritated at a
defense counsel, the Judge warned him he might face the
type of contempt citation that was once meted out to
attorneys representing Communist leaders. (Wall himself
made no insinuations of Communist sympathies on
anyone's part.) During a colloquy at the bench—not
included in the transcript—the Judge was heard to refer
to two priests who appeared as witnesses for Ferber as

"those so-called Roman Catholic priests." The transcript shows that in another bench conference, this one concerned with the admissibility as a witness of a young war resister described as having long hair, Judge Ford said, "I hope he has long hair." In several instances, he gave the impression of accepting the government's charge as fact, referring to it flatly as "this conspiracy" or "the conspiracy." The day before he gave the jury its instructions, he predicted during a bench conference, "There will be one verdict, and that will be guilty on [a] conspiracy count."

Dr. Spock and Ferber—the oldest and the youngest of the accused—probably adapted themselves best as defendants. Ferber's case was buttressed by the support of the two priests, and also by that of his roommate, who testified that when he himself was pondering whether to turn in his draft card during a church service at which Ferber was to deliver the sermon Ferber had counselled caution. "He stated he was very sympathetic with my own hesitancy to face the possible consequences of it," the roommate said. Ferber himself displayed poise on the stand, and his testimony was measured and economical. His duel with Wall was protracted, but at times it seemed that the two weren't really talking to each other, so dissimilar were their worlds. I was particularly struck by this dissimilarity when the prosecutor offered in evidence the text of Ferber's sermon last October before a congregation of young people, a hundred and fifty of whom, it turned out, were present to surrender their draft cards. Naturally, Wall offered the document as incriminating Ferber, yet someone else, with a different point of view, might, I thought, have seen it as anything but incriminating. Here are some excerpts:

> There is a great tradition within the church and synagogue which has always struggled against the conservative and worldly forces that have always been in control. It is a radical tradition, a tradition of urgent impulse to go to the

root of the religious dimension of human life. This tradition in modern times has tried to recall us to the best ways of living our lives: the way of love and compassion, the way of justice and respect, the way of facing other people as human beings and not as abstract representatives of something alien and evil. . . .

In religious terms, it is [a mistake] to dwell too much on the possibility of the Apocalypse; in political terms, it is [a mistake] to dwell too much on the possibility of a Utopian society. We must not confuse the ceremony and symbolism of today's service with the reality that we are only a few hundred people with very little power. And we must not confuse the change inside each of us, important though that may be, with the change that we have yet to bring about in this country and the world. Neither the Revelation nor the Revolution is at hand, and to base our hopes and plans on them would be a tragic blunder. . . .

It is not going to be easy to change this country. To change it is going to mean struggles and anguish day in and day out for years. It will mean incredible efforts at great human cost to gain a few inches of ground. It will mean people dedicating their lives and possibly losing them for a cause we can only partly define and whose outcome we can only guess at. We must say Yes to the long struggle ahead or this service will be a mockery. . . .

So then what are we to do? We must look at ourselves once more. We all have an impulse to purification and martyrdom and we should not be ashamed of it. But let us be certain that we have thought through the consequences of our action in the outside world and that these consequences are what we want to bring about. Let us make sure we are ready to work hard and long with each other in the months to come, working to make it difficult and politically dangerous for the government to prosecute us, working to help anyone and everyone to find ways of avoiding the draft, to help disrupt the workings of the draft and the armed forces until the war is over. Let us make sure we can form a community. Let us make sure we can let others depend on us.

It was the last paragraph that Wall concentrated on,

vigorously probing its rhetorical components for signs of conspiracy.

Q.: "Mr. Ferber, when you said toward the end of your speech on October 16, 1967, at Arlington Street Church, 'Let us make sure we are ready to work hard and long with each other in the months to come, working to make it difficult and politically dangerous for the government to prosecute us,' what did you mean by that? . . ."

A.: "One of the things I had in mind when I said that was political campaigning to end the war, that our example was a kind of petition to Congress to act, and that it might encourage candidates to run for office. . . ."

Q.: "And you are a great adherent of staying within the political system, using the ballot box to change things, are you?"

A.: "Among other things, yes."

Q.: "Among what other things?"

A.: "Among demonstrations and protests."

Q.: "Including civil disobedience?"

A.: "On occasion, yes."

Q.: "'Working to help anyone and everyone to find ways of avoiding the draft'—what did you mean by that?"

A.: "I meant that we, who are now in the Resistance [an anti-draft organization], who are not avoiding the draft, would help other people find legal ways to do so. . . ."

Q.: "You are not avoiding the draft, you are rejecting it completely, is that right?"

A.: "I am resisting it. . . ."

Q.: "'To help disrupt the workings of the draft and the armed forces until the war is over'—what did you mean by that?"

A.: "I meant that individuals would refuse on their own to cooperate with the draft system and the armed forces; that is, by conscientiously refusing to take part in it until the war was over."

Q.: "Individuals would refuse on their own?"

A.: "Yes, naturally. . . ."

Q.: "Without any attempt to convert them by you?"

A.: "To what position?"

Q.: "To refusing to go into the service?"

A.: "No, we have not been converting people to do that. . . ."

Q.: " 'Let us make sure we can form a community' —what did you mean by that?"

A.: "A number of things. I meant in particular that we should find ways to— well, to get to know one another better; to make sure that what we had done was not just an isolated act of protest but that our own personal lives would be improved; and that we would help—really comfort—each other in the trials that might come."

Two days after Dr. Spock's cross-examination ended, Wall, in his summation to the jury, saluted the celebrated physician for his forthrightness on the witness stand. Facing the dozen men, the prosecutor told them, "I submit to you you'd be warranted in finding that if he goes down in this case, he goes down like a man, with dignity, worthy of respect." In extolling Dr. Spock, the prosecutor may have been extolling himself as well, by calling attention to his intrepidity in jousting with so formidable an opponent, for in their confrontation the hunted often appeared the hunter; there were moments when, peering at his young inquisitor, the retired pediatrician seemed to be trying to place him as a tiny patient of long ago. Dr. Spock, a big, spare man, who once rowed No. 7 on the Yale crew, made a courtly, old-fashioned figure as he sat tall in his habitual dress—a dark-blue suit and a light-blue shirt with a high white collar. He spoke with earnest simplicity throughout. When he was asked whether there was any connection between his beliefs about the war and the field of pediatrics, he replied, "What is the use of physicians like myself trying to help parents to bring up children, healthy and happy, to have them killed in such numbers for a cause that is ignoble?"

Cross-examination brought out the fact that Dr. Spock did not approve of certain anti-war tactics. Among these were desertion to a neutral country and flight to Canada, which, he said, might solve an individual's own problem but wouldn't help end the war. Nor did Dr. Spock go along with sending money to the Vietcong or with destroying Selective Service files; he considered these "counterproductive in terms of public opinion." He gave patriotism as a motive for his anti-war activities, declaring that the waging of a war "that has no shred of legality . . . will blacken the reputation of my country for decades, if not centuries to come." Despite the solid-citizen ring of these replies, there was nothing skin-saving about Dr. Spock's testimony. He answered all questions, including hypothetical ones that he could have ignored. When Wall suggested that it was sheer chance that someone other than Dr. Spock had proffered the briefcase of turned-in draft cards to the official at the Justice Department, the physician replied that, whether or not this was so, he unreservedly backed the gesture. He readily admitted having advocated that middle-aged people take part in sit-ins; such support, he said, would help the morale of young demonstrators, who "feel lonely" when they are set upon by campus or city police. Nor did he show a moment's hesitation in affirming that he had once said, "Getting five hundred thousand men home from Vietnam justifies us in civil disobedience."

As was true in respect to the other defendants, practically all the evidence against Dr. Spock was culled from public sources. For instance, government research turned up an interview that Dr. Spock had given to the reporter of a local newspaper on landing at a South Carolina airport in November, 1967. In it he was quoted as saying, "I am not advocating violent civil disobedience, but I think those that are against the war should burn their draft cards and those that are in the military should refuse to go to Vietnam." Wall now wanted to know whether the quotation accurately reflected Dr.

Spock's views. "Approximately my views," he replied,
"but I come to my views very slowly and I express them
very carefully and I doubt very much that I said— What
was the verb in the last phrase?"

Q.: " 'Those that are in the military should refuse to go
to Vietnam.' "

A.: " 'Should refuse'—I would never say 'should
refuse.' Everyone has to make up his own mind. . . . I
hope that many men will refuse to be inducted and I hope
that many men will conclude that the war is illegal and
will refuse to obey orders, but that is not the same as
'should,' 'I think they should,' or that I urged them to."

The government did unearth an original piece of
evidence—an F.B.I. interview with Dr. Spock that took
place on December 8th, three days after the Whitehall
Street demonstration. Conducted by Agents George W.
Madison and George G. McKenna, the interview perhaps
constituted the only touch of detective-story atmosphere
in the entire trial, for in all other respects there was
essential accord on the facts presented, the disagreement
lying, of course, in the way they were interpreted. At that,
according to Dr. Spock's testimony, it was only one-quar-
ter of the F.B.I. interview that was in contention—the
matter of whether the agents had informed Dr. Spock that
their mission in seeing him was to discuss his possible
violation of the Military Selective Service Act of 1967. Dr.
Spock told Wall, "If there had been any such warning . . . if I had had any indication that they were . . .
collecting testimony to be used against me in court, I
would have immediately said I would end this discussion. . . ." As far as he was concerned, Dr. Spock
testified, the men wanted to hear about his "total
involvement in the peace movement"—an impression he
gained when Madison opened the questioning by asking,
"How did you get involved in all this?" Now, upon being
asked by Boudin why he had consented to see the F.B.I.
at all, Dr. Spock replied, "I wanted to be entirely
aboveboard. In spite of the fact that I was not required to

meet them, I wanted to show that I was ready to cooperate with any department of our government that wanted to talk with me, that I had nothing to hide." He did, however, consult a lawyer the night before his scheduled appointment, and although the lawyer's advice never came to light in court, it may have accounted for Dr. Spock's refusal to sign a document that the agents handed him soon after their meeting with him began. The document apprised him of his rights, which included silence, but, according to McKenna's notes, Dr. Spock returned it unsigned, saying, "No, I feel if I sign this form, there is an implication in my signature that whatever you gentlemen say I said in this interview I did in fact say."

McKenna's notes were crucial to both his testimony and Madison's. They were taken at a desk in the Spock apartment, in Manhattan. Madison, the ranking agent, who did practically all the interrogating, shared a sofa with Dr. Spock. Back at headquarters, later on, the agents collaborated on a report, but the notes were more often cited in court, both by Wall and by defense counsel. Dr. Spock denied an assertion in the notes that McKenna had read his statements back to him to check on whether they correctly reflected his views, one of which, according to the notes, was that he was attempting to "interfere with the raising of troops": "I deny that I used those words. They sound very legal or even out of the Constitution of the United States. I think those [words] and the others are Mr. McKenna's interpretation of what I was saying." There was an extended wrangle over whether Dr. Spock, on being asked to discuss his activities concerning the administration of the Selective Service system, had "thrown back his head and laughed" and said, "Telling you what I am telling you, I will be hanging myself, and I may wind up in jail." Questioned about this by Wall, Dr. Spock said, "That was a pleasantry in regard to the whole thing. I was aware the Federal Bureau of Investigation is an investigative body and they weren't there to make

friends with me. I was still willing to talk to them
frankly." Wall introduced items from the New York *Daily
News* and a C.B.S. telecast to support his suggestion that
Dr. Spock had aspired to a jail term. Disclaiming any
pretensions to martyrdom, the physician said, "I didn't
mean that I would be pleased to be prosecuted and I
certainly didn't mean that I myself ever sought prosecution. I meant that if the government chose to prosecute me
I would be glad to have this opportunity to prove that we
were right."

Boudin bore down hard on Madison, the attorney's
single objective being to demonstrate the shortcomings of
the interview as a piece of evidence. When Madison
testified that within five minutes after their arrival he and
McKenna had informed Dr. Spock of the purpose of their
visit, Boudin invited him to peruse the fifteen pages of
notes that McKenna had taken in the course of the
interview. Was there any mention on page 1 that the
purpose of the visit had been disclosed to Dr. Spock? Or
page 2? Or page 3? Each time, Madison replied, "It is not
there."

Q.: "In order not to spend more time, am I correct in
stating that nowhere . . . appears the statement which
you testified earlier you made to Dr. Spock as to the
reason for the investigation?"

A.: "Yes, sir."

Upon being asked whether it is customary for agents to
reveal the statute that the person interviewed is suspected
of having violated, Madison said, "Well, in this matter,
Dr. Spock through radio and television had openly stated
what he was doing."

Q.: "Who told you to visit him?"

A.: "It was on the orders of the Department of Justice."

Q.: "I see. And who in the Department of Justice?"

A.: "I don't know."

Q.: "Who gave you your orders?"

A.: "It came in on a communication from Washington."

Q.: "In writing?"

A.: "No, teletype. . . ."

Q.: "Did you think it was important that Dr. Spock had laughed when he said he was going to hang himself? Yes or no? . . ."

A.: "Yes. . . ."

Q.: "Why did you think it was important?"

A.: "I thought it kind of painted a general picture of how the situation was there."

Q.: "You mean his laughing or the remark he made about hanging?"

A.: "I think his laughing, and I think it was kind of typical of Dr. Spock—laughing."

Q.: "What do you mean that it was typical of Dr. Spock, that he was laughing?"

A.: "I thought it was just in the nature of which he did it, seemed just typically Dr. Spock."

Q.: "Typically?"

A.: "And treating it lightly."

Q.: "And did you treat it lightly?"

A.: "No."

Wall handled his summation well, forgoing his earlier tone of scandalized incredulity for one of calm reasonableness as he touched on the main aspects of the case for the jurors. He did occasionally permit himself a fustian moment, however. Having declared that the defendants practiced a "soft sell" on the gullible young, Wall recalled that he had first encountered this clever approach as a high-school student reading *Julius Caesar,* and the prosecutor then declaimed, " 'Friends, Romans, countrymen, lend me your ears;/I come to bury Caesar, not to praise him./The evil that men do lives after them,/The good is oft interred with their bones.' " Spelling out for the jury the full meaning of Mark Antony's famous lines, Wall said, "And [Antony] goes on to say what noble men Brutus and Cassius are and what a bad guy Caesar is. By the time he is finished with that speech, Brutus and

Cassius are running for their lives. He is still saying they are noble men, but the words have taken on an insidious effect—the soft sell."

In dealing with the question of why the five defendants had been indicted when hundreds, even thousands, of other co-conspirators might just as easily be standing trial, Wall drew what he termed "a poor analogy" with traffic speed traps, maintaining that the defendants were comparable to a speeder who asks why he is being given a ticket when five other drivers who were also speeding got away with it. Law enforcement serves as a deterrent, Wall told the jurors, and when enough speeders have been picked up, the word gets around to the rest. Concluding the analogy, he said, "If it's a real bad speed trap and real danger to the safety of the community, there comes a point where maybe you will have to have enough police out there to stop everybody who speeds."

Wall also felt constrained to debate the political views that the defendants had voiced in explaining the "state of mind" that had prompted their actions. Deriding the defendants as "intellectuals" and "great thinkers," and lumping himself with "us who are not that bright," he zeroed in on Raskin in particular, possibly because Raskin stood the best chance of escaping conviction. Why, the prosecutor demanded, did Raskin, "the head of some kind of brain factory in Washington," consider the Vietnam war illegal but the Korean war legitimate? Without mentioning selective conscientious objection, Wall asked what basis Raskin had for insisting that the Vietnamese war was illegal simply because Congress hadn't formally declared war. Hadn't the same been true of the Korean war? Then how did it happen that Raskin hadn't branded the earlier war equally illegal? Raskin's answer here, Wall recalled for the jury, was that the U.N. Security Council had ratified the Korean action. But, the prosecutor asked, did that mean that the Security Council had the power to commit American troops without any congressional declaration of war? He had posed the question to Raskin, Wall reminded the jurors, and hadn't they seen for themselves how it had stumped the expert from Washington?

As for the exercise of individual conscience, Wall depicted it as a potential undoer of "the collective conscience of the American people as expressed by the laws that are passed through our duly elected representatives." It would be wrong, he said, for the country to tie itself to an individual's conscience, "even to the conscience of a man as sincere and as dedicated and as great as Dr. Spock." The protesters might claim to be intellectuals, but "they don't think, they feel." "It's belly feel or gut reaction," the prosecutor declared. "They feel something is wrong or right. They feel it and they act on that feeling, on their conscience." He raised a series of questions designed to show that conscience and self-indulgence might well be synonymous. What about the Southern segregationist, whose Bible tells him integration is wrong—should he rely on his own conscience? What about the rich man who believes the tax laws are confiscatory? What about mothers on relief who find their checks too meagre—should they chain themselves to the doors of City Hall? Wall himself answered none of the questions, but it wasn't incumbent on him to do so. He did, however, declare himself on what the consequences of conscientious behavior were. "Anarchy," he said. "Every man a law to himself."

Judge Ford, in his charge to the jury, said that the flouting of law on the basis of belief "would permit every objector to become a law unto himself." Adhering to the indictment, he endeavored to isolate the charge of conspiracy from its alleged objectives, but as he discoursed on the flexible charge there were moments when it sounded as though the charge of conspiracy were an afterthought—as though the recognition of the crime must be preceded by the attainment of its objectives. Thus, describing conspiracy as "generally a matter of inference," Judge Ford instructed the jurors that "proof

of the accomplishment of an objective of a conspiracy is
the most persuasive evidence of the conspiracy itself."
However, the Judge also said, lack of success was no
proof of innocence. Mention was made of the First
Amendment's guarantees of freedom of speech and
assembly, but there was no exploration of whether the
defendants had believed that they were protected by their
constitutional rights in protesting the war. It was ruled
"no defense" that some defendants had protested in order
to bring about a test case, and in Judge Ford's opinion it
was "irrelevant and immaterial" that the accused had
made no attempt to conceal their activities from government agencies. The activities were always considered in
the light of the strictly criminal; in illustrating the
difference between motive and intent ("at times the
line . . . is not too easy to draw") he spoke of an
automobile thief who steals to improve the efficiency of a
benevolent-aid society. Judge Ford invariably referred to
the five defendants collectively, leaving their activities
undifferentiated. Addressing the jurors as "tryers of fact,"
he cautioned them not to be misled by "false trails and
issues," observing at one point that "we are not trying the
United States of America or President Johnson." And,
reiterating what had been his basic view throughout the
trial, the Judge told the twelve men, "There is no freedom
to knowingly conspire to violate a law of the United States
with impunity merely because one believes or doubts that
the law is immoral or illegal or unconstitutional, if the
law is within the constitutional power of Congress to
enact, which [the Military Selective Service Act of 1967]
is. The defendants here have testified that they believed
the war in Vietnam was immoral, illegal, and unconstitutional."

Once the jury had gone out to make its deliberations,
around noon, the courtroom emptied. Some of the
spectators retreated to the corridor for speculating
sessions of indefinite duration; others left the building for
good, believing that the jury would be out for more hours

than they cared to wait. As the time dragged by (it proved to encompass both lunch and dinner), people drifted back to see whether anything was stirring, but their numbers were never again sufficient to fill the courtroom. They seated themselves in the now relatively deserted rows and read, or they aimlessly wandered the aisles, or perhaps, in the new atmosphere, they finally shared smiles of recognition with other spectators, whom they might have been noticing for weeks.

When five or six hours of the vigil had passed, I joined Dr. Spock, who had cordially waved to me from a distance, indicating an unoccupied place beside him. He was sitting alone in the last row of the courtroom, far from his accustomed chair up front, and, in this anxious moment, he seemed disposed to talk. He was the same off the stand as on, his tone that of a man speaking his mind rather than that of a careful logician. I asked Dr. Spock only one question, and he took over from there. The question had to do with whether he was perhaps being "used"—that is, exploited—by peace groups who were out to advance special interests of their own. I had heard it raised repeatedly during the trial—in the pressroom, in the corridor, at lunch—by persons who considered themselves objective. Dr. Spock said that he knew the question well. "No, I'm not being used," he told me. "I'm doing what I believe needs to be accomplished. If peace people are using me, then I'm doing the same with them. Maybe I give the impression of being used because I dress so differently from the way many protesters do. And then there's my age—what's a sixty-five-year-old man doing running around with fifteen- and twenty-year-olds? I look conservative even when I'm with Wall Street financiers. Well, perhaps I do have a conservative side of my own. For example, I shrink back when I hear of protesters' chaining themselves inside induction centers. I couldn't ever do that. I even wonder how I do some of the things I do do—like taking part in that Whitehall Street demonstration. My whole upbringing cries out

against sitting on sidewalks or making an ass of myself
climbing police barriers. Oh, my awful conscience!" He
gave a mock groan. "It's the sternest sort of thing, always
lurking there underneath my mild manner." He laughed
at himself, saying he blamed his conscience for condemn-
ing him to a hectic retirement. A passionate sailor, he had
anticipated cruising in his ketch as much as three months
of the year, depending on whether his wife could take
that much; as New Yorkers, they had counted on seeing a
good deal of ballet; and then there were to have been
frequent visits with their children and grandchildren,
who lived in New England. But now those plans had
been disrupted. Just fighting the indictment, he said,
could take up all his time. But he was also working on two
books, one of which, he observed thoughtfully, might be
worthwhile for teen-agers to reflect on. "I think girls are
being encouraged to be too competitive with boys," he
said.

Turning his mind back to the trial, Dr. Spock said that
he had no desire to go to jail but that, in terms of the peace
movement, the indictment had thus far proved "a helpful
episode." Like Ferber, he thought that the movement was
regarded with less scorn now that the government had, so
to speak, accorded it official recognition. Since the
indictment, he said, he had been speaking before larger
audiences, for higher fees—the fees being turned over to a
defense fund for draft resisters—and he had been
receiving an ovation at the beginning and the end of his
speeches, which didn't use to be the case.

Three marshals entered the courtroom, and everyone
stopped talking, to see whether the small event forecast
the imminent return of the jury. But nothing happened;
the marshals merely seated themselves. Dr. Spock, too,
watched them for a moment. Then he said, smiling, "I
voted for Calvin Coolidge." Not until he had left New
Haven, his home town, to study medicine at Columbia
had he dreamed that any sensible voter could possibly be
anything but a Republican, he continued. He had voted

for Franklin D. Roosevelt, he recalled, and had been cut
by friends as a result. The trend of his political thinking
had steadily veered away from his conservative rearing,
until, in 1962, he landed in the peace movement.
"Ninety-nine per cent of my friends tell me to stop
behaving like a fool," Dr. Spock said. "But why should I
worry about them? They not only don't want to remake
the world, they don't even want to make money—that's
how retired they are." Any chance of saving the world,
Dr. Spock went on, rested not with "the country-club set"
but with the young. They were the idealistic and the
realistic ones, he said, and his voice grew enthusiastic as
he discussed their vitality and promise; one could easily
guess why he had become a pediatrician. He said he
would go wherever he could help the young preserve
themselves from the dangers of an unjustified war. It
gratified him to realize that he could lend encouragement
to youth, as he was constantly being told he could. How
could one possibly be "used" in allying oneself with the
young? They trafficked in trust, and he responded in
kind; it had always been that way in the course of his long
practice. "When I hear that talk of my being used," he
said, "I sometimes ask myself, 'Am I that ingenuous, am I
that uncertain of my views?' Perhaps some people think
I'm overly trusting, but that's not anything I want to give
up. It has helped me achieve whatever I have achieved,
and no matter what happens to me now I'm going to stay
that way."

It was early in the evening when word went out that the
jury was about to return, and in no time marshals,
reporters, and spectators were back in the courtroom.
Once the jury and Judge Ford were also in, the five
verdicts came fast, each elicited by the clerk's "Mr.
Foreman, what say you, is the defendant at the bar guilty
or not guilty?" All the defendants were found guilty
except Raskin, who was acquitted. He stood stunned and
stony-faced. Wearing smiles of rueful resignation, the
new convicts congratulated him and to an extent

themselves, for his acquittal attested to the imperfection of their alleged conspiracy—a point that might be of use in an appeal.

Three and a half weeks later, on July 10, 1968, Dr. Spock, Chaplain Coffin, Ferber, and Goodman were back in the Boston courtroom to hear Judge Ford pass sentence upon them. Outside the Federal Building, huge picket lines were in full cry, shouting peace slogans, and a few counter-pickets warned of the dangers of Communism and civil rights. The courtroom was soon filled with spectators—among them, I noticed, Raskin, who sat down unobtrusively in a back row. After every place was taken, Colonel Paul F. Feeney, the deputy director of Selective Service in Massachusetts, arrived, resplendent in a beribboned Army uniform. Smiling indiscriminate greetings, he proceeded to a chair that some marshals had hurriedly produced. Just before Judge Ford's entrance, I asked Colonel Feeney why he had come, and he replied, "The sentencing today is the climax of a case in which we have been interested, and my presence here is an expression of that interest."

Judge Ford made a few remarks before passing sentence. He said that the government had accused the four men of "what amounts to rebellion against the law," and then he quoted a Southern judge who had said in 1835, "Rebellion against the law is in the nature of treason." Judge Ford said that "the intellectual as well as all others" must be deterred from lawlessness, or we would face "anarchy." Young men were being sent to jail every week for evading military service, he went on, and it would be "preposterous" for those who had, "as the jury found, conspired to incite" them to evade it "to escape under the guise of free speech." He then sentenced each of the men to two years in prison and fined each of them except Ferber five thousand dollars; Ferber was fined one thousand.

The sentenced men were released on their own recognizance pending an appeal, and they left the

building together, to attend a press conference at a hotel a
block or two away. As they emerged into the street, the
peace pickets broke their lines and swarmed about the
four men, cheering and chanting slogans. The swirling
crowd made it difficult for television crews and photographers to take pictures of them. Raskin, I saw, walked
alongside them. It was a narrow street, and progress
toward the hotel was very slow, as one could easily tell by
watching Dr. Spock's forward motion—his stalwart frame
towered above the crowd. I could see no police around,
but the surging mob of pickets never got out of hand; they
seemed at home in the streets, where their movement was
born. I pushed my way over to Raskin, whose manner was
lively and impatient; he had apparently accepted his fate
as a free man. Raising his voice above the din, he told me
that he, too, was on his way to the press conference,
where he would share the platform with the rest of the
Boston Five.

"Why did you come back?" I asked.

"How could I *not* have come back?" he shouted.

2

OUT OF IT

🏴 🏴 🏴 🏴 🏴

The longer the undeclared war in Asia went on, the more apparent it was that other Americans, like Dr. Spock and his co-defendants, were questioning the government's right to ask them to bear arms. When the first of America's armed "advisers" set foot in Vietnam, during President Eisenhower's first administration, military service was largely an unchallenged institution, but with the lengthening of the controversial war even the straightest of America's young men thought twice about heeding Uncle Sam's call to the colors. Thousands of them had taken to resisting the draft after 1967 but what was more startling perhaps was that large numbers of those already in uniform were resorting to desertion. More than seventy thousand desertions—illegal absences from military duty for more than thirty days—occurred in one twelve-month period for which the Defense Department gave out figures. Again according to the Defense Department, "most" deserters returned voluntarily. But many did not, thereby

risking sentences of up to five years in the stockade at
hard labor; were the war one that had been conventional-
ly declared by Congress, deserters would have been
subject to the death penalty.

Many of the deserters went underground in the United
States, moving from one hiding place to another. Others
became expatriates, finding haven abroad, notably in
Canada and Sweden. In Canada, there were far more draft
resisters than there were deserters, but in Sweden, which
I visited in the fall of 1969, deserters had been
predominant since 1967, when Sweden granted asylum to
the first of the disaffected servicemen—four sailors off the
aircraft carrier *Intrepid,* who had jumped ship in Japan
and then, to Russian cheers, crossed the Soviet Union.
Since the arrival of the Intrepid Four, as the sailors
became known, a colony of outlaw exiles from all
branches of the armed forces had gradually grown up in
Sweden. Talking with numerous deserters, as well as
American Embassy people and Swedish government
officials, I gathered that their ranks came to roughly four
hundred. Nobody would venture an exact figure. For one
thing, it was pointed out to me, there was no keeping
track of the number of loners earning their livelihood as
miners and lumberjacks in isolated settlements along the
Arctic Circle. Then, too, the deserter population varied
when its members, indulging an impulse toward wander-
lust, drifted on to some other European country.
Occasionally, a deserter turned himself in at the
American Embassy in Stockholm. The size of the colony
also changed constantly with the steady but unpredictable influx of military immigrants, some of whom, I
learned, had already inspected Sweden as a prospective
haven while on leave from their units; one deserter and
his wife had arrived with a working knowledge of
Swedish, having studied the language while he was at
camp in California. The feelings of the young men on
reaching Swedish soil were often a mixture of elation and
uncertainty. In reading a diary loaned to me by one of

them, an infantryman who had been decorated in
Vietnam, I came upon the following entry: "Freedom at
last! I'm in Sweden now on the train to Stockholm. I feel
at the top of the world. My new home, my new country.
May I be happy here! People take me for a Swede. That is
good—when I learn the language, life here will be easier
for me."

With few exceptions, the men were alone when they
reached Sweden, for their decisions to desert were the
result of solitary ruminations in America, Germany, and
Asia. As for organized political activity, this seemed to
begin in Sweden, more or less as an afterthought. From
what I could ascertain, it was only a minority of the
deserters who sought political expression, and their
principal outlet, the American Deserters Committee, was
an impoverished group racked by confusion and dissen-
sion. While its leaders sounded Maoist in viewpoint, the
organization had generally proved itself less an ideological force than a fraternal lodge, its good works consisting
in helping deserters get their bearings in an alien land.
Discussing the organization with me, Mrs. Kristina
Nystrom, who saw nearly all deserters in her capacity as
kurator of Sweden's Immigration and Naturalization
Board, said that she frequently counted on the A.D.C.'s
assistance. "I don't consider it a political act to ring
them," she said. "There's always someone there who'll go
fetch some deserter for me—some bewildered boy who
hasn't picked up a welfare check, or kept an appointment
for a job opening, or perhaps with a doctor who can help
him cut out drugs. The majority of deserters I see feel
deserted themselves, especially those who tell me their
parents won't have anything more to do with them."

Some deserters were fairly well-heeled their first days
in Sweden, thanks to having employed such last-minute
ruses as negotiating Army loans or collecting reenlistment
bonuses; one deserter I encountered had left his tank unit
in Germany with a hundred dollars that an officer had
given him as a farewell gift. The men were usually broke,

however, which was not an unfamiliar state for most of
them, since, as Mrs. Nystrom found, they were preponderantly volunteers from small towns who had signed up
out of economic need. Only two or three of the dozens of
deserters I talked with were college graduates, and, in
sharp contrast to campus draft resisters, all of the
deserters told me that before enlisting they had had only
the haziest notion of the issues at stake in the war. Even
while maintaining that their own opposition to the
war—based on actual military experience—was unquestionably more authoritative than that of "just book
readers," several of them betrayed a certain envy of draft
resisters. Referring to them, a recent artillery sergeant told
me, "They didn't have to throw away a uniform, the way I
did. Once you do that, it's like a sin. It sticks with you that
maybe you've done something wrong to get out of it, no
matter how wrong the war itself is."

The deserters were not an easygoing group. Cast in the
un-American role of refugee, they were hard pressed, as
immigrants always have been, to gain a foothold in a
foreign country. It made an oddly disconcerting sight, I
found, to watch them queue up with huddled masses of
tired, hungry-looking Greeks, Czechs, Hungarians, and
Yugoslavs in a gloomy police station to cope with
immigration red tape. Attracted to Sweden by its
reputation as a welfare state, the ex-servicemen depended
heavily on the government for medical care, tuition
grants, housing allowances, and other benefits—all told,
about a hundred and thirty dollars a month, a sum that
left the deserters scrambling for a marginal livelihood.
The bulk of them divided their time between attending
school and holding down such menial jobs as dishwash-
ers, garbage collectors, and, in one instance, a household
servant; one of the Intrepid Four, when I was in Sweden,
worked as a janitor in a factory that turned out frozen
French-fries. The most educated deserter I talked with
was a Columbia Law School graduate, class of 1967, and
he was studying to be a programmer in a computing firm.

A former Republican Party worker in a Brooklyn precinct, he told me sardonically that it was too bad his training was going to waste, since American lawyers were both needed and scarce in Sweden. "I could help people at the U.S. Embassy file tax returns, but I'm not counting on it," he said.

Along with refugees from other countries, the Americans attended language schools for at least two months, their studies underwritten by the government, on the theory that the sooner outlanders learned Swedish the sooner they would be able to support themselves. The schools operated on a five-day week, each day lasting six hours, and the atmosphere in the classes was likely to be on the sombre side. "It's a break with your past to have to study that language," one deserter told me. "All of us sit there knowing full well that only trouble could have driven us to neutral Sweden." Fortunately for many deserters, they were popular with Swedish girls, whose quarters were often the men's solution to the general housing shortage in Sweden. Occasionally, I was told, the relationships between the deserters and girls matured, but when they didn't the deserter was likely to feel a sharp sense of dislocation. "Breaking up with a girl here isn't the same as doing it back home," a twenty-five-year-old Midwesterner told me. "When it happens here, you start asking yourself all over again where in the world it is that you really belong."

Perhaps the colony's most discernible sign of wariness was its guarded treatment of outsiders, for the suspicion was widespread among deserters that, through one trick or another, the United States government was bent on spiriting them from their safe ground into captivity. At the United States Embassy, officials ridiculed this fear, while freely admitting to me that they were empowered to pay the fare of "absentees" willing to return to American jurisdiction. Even among Swedes, however, the feeling persisted that security agents, Swedish or American, might be infiltrating the colony. Mrs. Nystrom, for

example, informed me that her countrymen found it
mysterious, early in 1969, when mail from America
reached deserters who, for one reason or another, were
trying to keep their whereabouts secret; the mail was from
parents imploring their sons to abandon their criminal
existence.

Given the suspicion of outsiders, I might have had
considerable difficulty in meeting deserters had it not
been for the good offices of Father Thomas Lee Hayes, a
thirty-seven-year-old Episcopal priest, who was in Sweden, with his wife and two young daughters, as an
emissary of Clergy and Laymen Concerned About
Vietnam, an anti-war organization. A portly man with
hazel eyes that gleamed sympathetically from behind
rimless glasses, Father Hayes, who wore a peace cross of
his own design, had been sent to minister to the needs of
what he called "the parish over the hill." His mission, he
told me at our first meeting, reflected the recognition of
many churchmen that deserters had become "one of the
costs of the war." But in the course of the half year he had
thus far spent in Sweden, he said, it had become plain to
him that something other than a charitable impulse was
now required in dealing with the phenomenon of
deserters. They were continuing to cross borders in
increasing numbers, he said, and sooner or later they
would have to be either shunned as rank outlaws, like the
handful of thieves and pushers in their midst, or looked
upon as belated conscientious objectors—as though they
they had never donned uniforms. Father Hayes thought
that the deserters, for all their youthful confusion,
indigence, political callowness, and outlaw state, were
causing people everywhere to think anew about the
nature of patriotism. No anti-American plot accounted for
their defection. He said he knew this from long talks with
the men, who told him, in different ways, that their
military experience did not tally with their conception of
"the truly American." In every instance, Father Hayes
said, arduous self-examination had preceded desertion.

He spoke theologically. "The quality of surprise is once again at work," he said. "The presence of spirit in history again makes contact with men through their conscience. It leads them to face up to what they consider evil, regardless of danger. That is what the whole Biblical witness is about."

Father Hayes didn't often speak in a theological vein. He was perpetually occupied with the deserters' immediate, quite mundane needs, which he attended to not only in his office, a small, oblong room over a narrow street in Stockholm's Old City, but also in his apartment, which was open house for deserters. Between these two points, he was in motion a good part of the day carrying out errands of one sort of another in a balky Volvo, an expiring contraption that a smooth-talking deserter had conned him into buying. While I was in Sweden, he made several trips to the airport, an hour's drive from the capital, to pick up musical instruments for deserters who wanted to form rock groups; he had prevailed upon friends in the States to provide the instruments. He had also exhorted American tourists to come bearing foods that the deserters missed—soul food and peanut butter, bagels and Fig Newtons. Much of Father Hayes' time was given to relieving homesickness. It was rampant; the men turned out in force, for example, at any movie that afforded sweeping views of America. Father Hayes visited deserters who had suffered mental breakdowns, and on two occasions last summer he was called in after deaths. One of them was the suicide of a deserter who lived by himself on an island in the Baltic, and the other the accidental drowning of a twenty-one-year-old Texan named Greg. Perhaps exhilarated by the steady effulgence of a midnight sun, Greg and some friends had piled into a rowboat moored near a footbridge in Stockholm; the boat was caught in an eddy and capsized, its hull striking his head. Father Hayes had arranged for Greg's Swedish fiancee, Nita, a reserved, dark-eyed brunette, to accompany the body to Texas. I met her one evening at the Hayes

apartment, and she told me of her journey. Greg's father
had adamantly refused to believe his son had been a
deserter. Repudiating Nita's account, he had insisted that
Greg's drowning had not been accidental but the result of
an enemy agent's guile. "He told everyone Greg had been
with the C.I.A.," Nita said. "There was no use my saying
how Greg had changed in Europe, how in Germany he
had becomes a deep believer in non-violence, and how in
my country he had given himself to writing poetry and
stories. No, I cannot say I liked Greg's home town, but it
showed me how much it is possible for a human being to
grow."

Evenings, there were always a dozen or so visitors at
the Hayes apartment—young men at loose ends who
dropped in to have coffee and talk or read American
publications. Some of the deserters would arrive with
new girl friends to introduce to the Hayes family.
Explaining this regular attendance at his home, Father
Hayes told me, "Stockholm isn't much of a town for
hangouts, and the fellows like to come to a place where
they can hear English." His evenings were often marked
by phone calls concerning deserters, and on one occasion
when I was present he left his guests abruptly on hearing
that a member of his parish, a drug addict, had been jailed
for an attempted holdup. Father Hayes told me later that
similar incidents had taken place previously and inevitably attracted press attention that disparaged all deserters,
despite the fact that, according to Mrs. Nystrom, drug
addiction was no more prevalent among them (or among
U.S. soldiers still on duty) than among Swedish contemporaries. However, that was of no moment to the native
population, most of whom had misgivings about the
strangers settling in their midst. Their presence made
businessmen nervous about the future of commercial
relations with America, but, more broadly, the deserters
were a source of confusion, because Swedes were
accustomed to receiving refugees from the East, not the
West. "We think of America as the very opposite of

Russia," a hotel manager told me. "Many of us have
family in America. We think of it as a place of freedom."

In keeping with this reluctance to equate the American
government with dictatorships, exiles from Russia and
the Balkans were almost automatically granted "political
asylum," which protected them from deportation, while
the deserters were accorded "humanitarian asylum,"
which did not—the clear implication being that if the
occasion arose America, unlike one-party states, would
deal understandingly with her aberrant children. Apparently, the Swedes drew a distinction between the United
States as "a place of freedom" and as a prosecutor of the
war. In a Swedish poll in 1968, more than eighty-three per
cent of those canvassed were in favor of America's immediate withdrawal from Vietnam. Large anti-war demonstrations had been held at which deserters were fêted as heroic
fighters for peace. In the privacy of Swedish homes,
though, deserters were not necessarily cherished for their
heroism—a quality that Swedes were able to judge with
detachment, having avoided all wars, whether just or
unjust, for nearly two centuries. The noted economist
Professor Gunnar Myrdal, a highly publicized opponent
of the war, spoke belittlingly of the deserters, even while
conceding he had had scarcely any contact with them.
"They should have stayed home and fought for their
convictions, and if necessary gone to prison," he told me
in his office at Stockholm University. "I think the average
deserter here is not very bright, not cultivated, but then
one needn't be very bright to get out of a war."

In Father Hayes' office, the press of business was even
greater than at his apartment. When a new deserter
wandered in, his sole luggage perhaps a gas-mask bag
into which he had stuffed a few odds and ends, Father
Hayes dropped everything to find him a bed for the night,
warned him that Sweden might be a haven but was no
heaven, and informed him of Mrs. Nystrom and the
country's welfare system. His very attentiveness seemed
to relax the new arrivals, who were generally on edge.

When he introduced me as a journalist to one of them, an enormous, hulking Green Beret who had fled Vietnam, the man, whose home was in Ridgefield Park, New Jersey, thrust his passport at me and said, "Here's my picture, my number. Tell the world I've deserted." He made much of his passport. It had been issued him in four hours in New York, he said, when he had convinced the clerk that his sister lay dying in Brussels. And before that he had been given an emergency home furlough by getting his mother to wire him overseas that she was dying. He had been wounded twice, as a corporal with the Fifth Special Forces Group, for which, among other things, he had acted as an interpreter; the son of a French-Canadian father, he spoke French, as did many Vietnamese. He had had his fill of the Army, he said, after watching ten soldiers in his unit dismember a nine-year-old girl and her father. His voice needlessly loud, he said, "Politics are a fake. Be nice to people—that's the way to be."

It was in Father Hayes' office that I met a twenty-four-year-old fugitive from a Signal Corps unit near Frankfurt who told me that a week after he reached Sweden, in February, 1968, a former lieutenant of his called him up from Germany to try to negotiate his return. "I was flabbergasted," the deserter said. He was Robert A. Agento, of Miami, Florida, a bearded, thin-featured former sergeant, who theorized that the lieutenant must have learned his phone number from a soldier to whom he had written while he was living with a hospitable Swedish family that was seeing him through his first weeks in Stockholm. "The call made me feel right about having split." he said. "I'd done it to stop playing the Army game of compromise from one day to the next. I'd had two and a half years of that, and it was wrecking whatever idealism I had in me. Well, along comes this phone call to Sweden, and all it is is an invitation to play more compromise. The lieutenant tells me that if I come back within thirty days I can keep my grade. All that will happen to me is that I'll lose two-thirds of my month's

pay, or a hundred and seventy dollars. He'll even meet me
at the airport. I don't want to be impolite to him, so I join
in the bargaining. Who has authorized this offer, I ask,
and he answers that the commanding general has given it
a verbal O.K. Me: Send it in writing to me or my parents.
The lieutenant: I don't know whether we can do that. Me:
Maybe we should try. The lieutenant: Take my word for
it, as an officer and a gentleman. Me: But the guys upstairs
might be liars. After that, the lieutenant gave me his home
phone number and told me to call him collect if I changed
my mind."

Father Hayes was reluctant to generalize about the
deserters, but he did say that those who had been
stationed outside Vietnam appeared to decide on desertion only after learning they were headed for the war
zone. Naturally, he said, this could give an impression
that they were fleeing military service solely to save their
skins, but the impression would be quite wrong, for their
motives were many-faceted, as I would see for myself in
talking with the men. And it was most assuredly
untenable, he added, to associate desertion in general
with skin-saving, at least in relation to the Vietnam war.
There were infantrymen in Sweden with outstanding
combat records, among them a wounded Negro Marine
by the name of Terry Whitmore, who had been decorated
by President Johnson himself on one of his visits to
Vietnam. (Whitmore had made up his mind to quit after
watching a television newscast on the assassination of
Martin Luther King, Jr., in Memphis, Whitmore's home
town.) Getting back to deserters who had not been in
Vietnam, Father Hayes told me of one man who had come
to Sweden from the Edgewood Arsenal, in Maryland, on
hearing that he was to proceed to Vietnam with fifty
Dobermans he had just finished training for guard duty.
"Maybe his was a case of snobbery," Father Hayes
suggested. He said that another deserter—a West Point
graduate, no less, in the class of 1968—was a likable,
serious lieutenant, with ramrod posture and close-

cropped hair, who turned up in Stockholm after abandoning his post at Fort Benning, Georgia. As a cadet, Father Hayes told me, the young man had done a senior thesis on the constitutionality of the war, and his research had left him with so many doubts that on being ordered to Vietnam he had decided to go somewhere and meditate about the future of his military career. He remained in Stockholm five or six weeks, then went down to the Embassy one afternoon and arranged for his return. "He didn't want any part of the war, but he decided he had a commitment," Hayes said. "The last I heard of him, he was back at Benning."

Many deserters came from Germany, just across the Baltic, Father Hayes went on. One of them, a Midwesterner who had been trained for "pacification duty" in Vietnam, came to Sweden three weeks after his unit, as part of its training, was assembled to listen to a former Nazi officer lecture in a thick accent on "effective methods of administering detention camps." In March of 1968, Father Hayes told me, a military policeman on night duty at Checkpoint Charlie, in West Berlin, had ended a five-year Army career by the simple expedient of stepping over to the East Berlin side. He was a noncommissioned officer with the 287th M.P. detachment, who had a German wife and an infant son. Astounded at seeing him on their side of the barrier, his East German counterparts, all of whom he knew, passed him on to their superiors, who invited him to issue a denunciation of the United States. He refused. He wanted only to reach Sweden and live there with his family. He now did, Father Hayes said, in a town a hundred miles south of Stockholm, where he worked in a paper mill. After rummaging in his desk drawer, Father Hayes handed me a long letter from the deserter, in which I read, "I could never consider myself as being a political type person. My lack of education has limited my knowledge of such matters. However, I do not think that it requires an exceptionally bright person to understand what my

government wishes to do in the bloodbath that it is
carrying out in Viet Nam. . . . I have a quiet anger in
these matters and the best thing I have been able to do is
refuse my services to the U.S. Army in this act of
aggression."

One of the deserters with whom I spoke extensively
was Steven Gershater, a high-school droupout from New
York, whom I met in Father Hayes' office, where
Gershater had called to say goodbye. He was leaving for
Lapland the following morning, after living in Stockholm
since his desertion, in late April, 1968. We talked in an
outdoor cafe nearby, even though there was an autumn
chill in the air. Gershater wanted to watch the afternoon's
waning light. "Where I'll be this winter, the night lasts
twenty-three hours," he said. He was a short, genial man
of twenty-two, large-nosed, with blue-gray eyes and
brown hair that was moderately long. His mind was on
his impending departure. He could never have contem-
plated going to an Arctic outpost, he said, when he first
came to Sweden. He had then very much wanted to be
near other deserters, who were intensely clannish. "Those
were the Mayflower days," he said. "If we heard a new
deserter was due in, there'd be a group of us out at the
airport to greet him. We were an aristocracy—we'd call
ourselves No. 10 or 19, or whatever, to show in what order
it was that each of us had got here." Evidently, Gershater
went on, smiling, he had ridden out this stage, judging by
his readiness to become the northernmost deserter in
Sweden. "Somebody gave me an axe for a going-away
present," he said. In Lapland, he would live in a town of
two hundred, whose housing was primitive but whose
central ornament was a special school that stressed the
study of economics in different countries. Gershater
wanted to learn about socialism and imperialism and
other ideas that he had often heard fellow-deserters
bandy about. He suspected that they knew no more about
such matters than he did, but nevertheless he had held

back on entering discussions. Speaking earnestly, as though grading himself, he said, "I think I've reached the point where I can present my views on the shortcomings of capitalism." On attaining military age, he recalled, he had confessed his ignorance of world affairs to his father, a tailor in Greenwich Village. The father had responded. "When I was eighteen, I didn't worry about the President."

Gershater told me that when he reported to camp at Fort Rucker, Alabama, early in 1967, he had assumed that idealism motivated his government's participation in the war. But he could find no signs of any such idealism. Repeatedly, he said, military indoctrinators had lectured that the war was being fought for "the glory of America," which had sounded vague to his ears. He had attended Army films that impressed him as simpleminded, their footage depicting the enemy as bad and our troops as good. For a time, Gershater said, he had tried to persuade himself that the South Vietnamese forces were underdogs, but it had been a hard thing to believe. "All of us knew the amount of stuff we were pouring into Asia," he said. Nor had his duties imparted a sense of idealism. He had been assigned to run the camp's bowling alleys, in which capacity he was permitted to wear civilian clothes. Now and then, a uniformed bowler would ask whether he was in the service, and Gershater would lie. "I didn't want to hurt morale," he said. "I had the cushiest job in camp."

Shipped to Germany later in 1967 as a member of the 24th Division, Gershater remained acutely aware of his unsatisfied quest. Toward the end of 1967, his division was ordered to Fort Riley, Kansas, an established way station for outfits going to Vietnam, and Gershater knew that his moment of truth was at hand. Others must have felt the same, he thought, for once the division's orders became known there was an outbreak of ostensibly facetious remarks about hightailing it for Sweden. Recalling the mood around him, Gershater said, "The

fellows were in that in-between phase when they might
make up their minds one way or the other. In the end,
they let the Army do it for them."

"Were you afraid of being killed?" I asked.

Gershater replied, "That could be, but I was even more
afraid of doing the killing. It's not right for one person to
tell another to kill, especially when he sees no cause for it.
The thing I really stewed about was whether clearing out
would be just an act of self-indulgence. I had to convince
myself that it was O.K. for anyone to desert, not just for
Steven Gershater."

A month before the division pulled out of Germany,
Gershater received fourteen days' leave, nine of which he
spent in England, where he had relatives. He took his
remaining time in Stockholm, both to look over the
terrain and, equally important, to grant himself a final
respite in which possibly to change his mind. "But I
knew I wouldn't," he said, studying the leaden glint that
passed for Stockholm's autumn sun. "In or out of the
Army, I had to lose, and today there's nothing I can do but
accept the consequences of my desertion. I'm out of step
with my country's authorities, and my life is confused. I
miss Americans. I can't go to the place in the world I
know best, where my family lives, where I grew up."
Speaking impatiently, as though seeking to rout any
semblance of self-pity, Gershater told me, "But I'm not
saying I lost out on my ambitions. I hadn't yet developed
any. I was nineteen when I went in, so I hadn't yet seen
for myself the kinds of opportunities that can determine
what you do with your life. Maybe something wonderful
will happen in Lapland."

Unlike Gershater, John Toler, a tall, thin, yellow-haired
former Green Beret sergeant from the Far West, had little
urge to leave Stockholm. He had established a serious
relationship with a handsome Swedish girl and his
existence appeared to be generally well ordered. He lived
in a neat, modest apartment in a walkup in the Old City,

and on the walls of his study there were snapshots of his parents. They were planning to visit him in the summer, Toler said, which was a pleasant surprise. "They couldn't have expected me to do what I did," he said. "My father used to be a naval officer." Toler's study table was strewn with several books on philosophy, his field of concentration at Stockholm University; in America, he had left Oregon State University as a sophomore in order to enlist. His Swedish, Toler went on, was now good enough for him to envision becoming a teacher in his new country. Occasionally, he said, he experienced an intense craving for his mother's cooking and for certain forms of progressive rock, but otherwise he was content to go on sinking his roots in Sweden. He didn't want to return to the United States; nor was he interested in amnesty, for which other deserters were campaigning. Early in 1969, he told me, he had openly opposed the leadership of the American Deserters Committee, whose disposition he felt was to impose political discipline on all deserters; Toler organized a group called the Underground Railway, devoted to helping each man develop a life of his own among Swedes.

Toler put in a year and a half with the Special Forces, all of it at Fort Bragg, North Carolina. As an unpolitical nineteen-year-old, Toler said, he was highly susceptible to "the John Wayne myth" that lent glamour to the outfit. Besides, Toler added, qualifying for the Green Berets offered a number of unmythical advantages, among them better pay and faster promotion than were forthcoming in ordinary branches of the service. In addition, Toler said, the work itself was more interesting than routine training. There were all sorts of schools one could attend as a Green Beret, and among those he himself went to were parachute school, which he liked, and the John F. Kennedy Special Warfare School, where he learned, among other things, how to make a printing press out of berry juice and cheesecloth. Everybody was on a big school kick, Toler said, and for good reason. "The longer

you kept going to schools, the closer you got to civilian
life," he told me. "Except for a few officers, nobody I met
wanted to go to Vietnam. Certainly the returnees from
there didn't talk up the place. All they came back with
was shoptalk—tips, for instance, on which camps to avoid
because they were easy for Charlie to overrun. And when
the tough old sergeants—the career-oriented E-7s—got
drunk, they'd say things like 'You can dump 'Nam in the
ocean.' There just didn't seem to be anything over there
worth dying for. In my father's war, there was. I can
imagine fighting in that one. I may be a deserter, but I'm
no pacifist."

Reverting to his life at Fort Bragg, Toler, like
Gershater, said that he had failed to find a shining
justification for his activities, some of which consequent-
ly took on an absurd quality. He learned to play the bass
drum for the Special Forces Drum and Bugle Corps.
Under orders, he and other Green Berets honored Walter
Cronkite, a visiting V.I.P., by jumping from helicopters.
Driving a two-and-a-half-ton truck, Toler backed into a
passenger car, for which, as punishment, he was made
head of the motor pool. Then, there was an elaborate
guerrilla-warfare problem on which he was dispatched to
the bayou country of Louisiana. "We were liberating
Louisiana," Toler began, suppressing a smile. A civil war,
it appeared, was in progress, and Texans (in the form of
an Army division) were occupying a section of bayous
that Louisianians (Toler and other Green Berets) were out
to free; Cuban exiles were advising the Texans. Actually,
Toler said, a real civil war was going on, but it wasn't
supposed to be noticed. "We couldn't have blacks on our
team," he explained. "The farmer who was renting us his
acreage wouldn't have it. No 'niggras'—not while he paid
taxes."

Toler's unit received its Vietnam orders late in 1967,
and the men went on leaves of forty-five days. Within that
time, Toler knew, he had to face up to the doubts he had

been harboring. He was tempted to talk things out with his parents, but he felt that wouldn't be fair to them—whatever decision he reached, it had to be his own. He flew to San Francisco, where, dressed in civilian clothes, he spent time with anti-war protesters. They had little to teach him. He was beyond slogans. When he did come to his decision, Toler believed, it would be the product of the "sense impressions" he had accumulated in his daily life as a Green Beret.

"Were you afraid of being killed?" I asked.

Toler shook his head. In fact, he said, when he saw himself in Vietnam, it wasn't as a corpse but as the holder of a safe job, far from combat. "I had to ask myself whether that was what I wanted," Toler said. "The question led me straight to what I think of as moral considerations. Sure, I decided, I'd stay alive if I had safe duty, but it would leave me a weaker person, just floating, drifting. The real cop-out would be to stay in."

From San Francisco, he drove to New York in a rented car. "More sense impressions," he said. "What a country! It's got fantastically beautiful places—more beautiful than anything here in Sweden. Crossing the continent, I must have talked with a hundred people—gas attendants, carhops, hitchhikers, truckers having coffee. The war didn't bother them too much. It made me wonder just what it was I would be defending if I did go to Vietnam." In New York, he stayed with some people whose names he had been given out West. He applied for a passport, which he received in a few days—about a week after he was due back at Fort Bragg. His mind was made up, Toler said, but he didn't know *how* made up it was until a friend informed him that a man making a documentary film about the war was looking for a soldier to speak his piece. Toler reported to a private home, where he heard himself declare in front of a camera and microphone that he was going to desert. After that, he was in a big hurry to use his passport. He did, that very evening, at a time when New York was in the throes of a garbage strike. "The city reeked," Toler said. "I think I was in a state of moral ecstasy when I boarded the plane. It was going to land in Sweden February 10, 1968—the same day I was due in Vietnam."

In Uppsala, a historic seat of Lutheranism, fifty miles northwest of Stockholm, I talked with a devout Catholic, a former corporal at Fort Jackson, South Carolina, who had deserted with the utmost reluctance. "All my officers knew I didn't want to desert," he told me. The deserter was Patrick Downey, a tall, lithe, mild-mannered man whose home was in Copiague, Long Island, where he had earned his high-school letter in four sports. He was now a student of sociology at Uppsala University, having enrolled there shortly after he and his wife and infant son had reached Sweden in October, 1968. They had a pleasant three-room apartment in a building given over to student families, and it was there that Downey and I talked. Things were fairly well in hand, he said, thanks in part to the fact that his wife, Linda, was holding down a job teaching English in a Swedish kindergarten. He preferred the relaxed atmosphere of Uppsala, a college town that had a Catholic church, to that of Stockholm. During the summer, he remarked, American tourists who visited Uppsala had made a point of seeking out deserters, plying them with questions. On the whole, Downey said, the tourists had been more curious than anything else, but in the fall a contingent of collegians from California had come to spend their junior year at Uppsala, and they had been openly hostile. "I used to feel the same way about deserters," Downey said.

Downey had majored in physical education at North Texas State University, where he had met Linda, a beautiful Texan, who arrived home from her teaching job at the end of our talk, as I was leaving. It was in his senior year, shortly after Linda had become pregnant, that events had crowded in on him, rattling him hard, since, in

his words, he had been complacent about the war. Two
months shy of turning overage for the draft, Downey
heard from his board that he was 1-A. He moved at once
to control his situation as best he could, taking it up with
a recruiting sergeant. Downey wanted to finish school, get
a good job in the Army, and stay out of Vietnam, all of
which the sergeant had said could be guaranteed if he
would enlist for three years instead of being drafted for
two. Downey agreed. "I never even knew the sergeant's
name," Downey said. In August, 1967, now a college
graduate, Downey had reported to Fort Jackson, where in
a matter of days he had come into conflict with the Army.
It happened when Downey informed his captain that he
would never kill anyone, so there was little point in his
learning how to handle weapons, a standard part of the
eight-week basic training that everyone was expected to
take. "I seemed to confuse the captain," Downey told me.
"He promised that the Army would help me out but said
that he would appreciate it if I went ahead in the
meantime with basic training." Downey agreed, but
when nothing happened after this period he started
seeing chaplains. All of them gave varying estimates of
the number of years he would have to serve in prison if he
persisted in abjuring weapons. The most discouraging
chaplain was a Catholic, who held that anyone who
bucked for conscientious-objector status after joining the
Army must be out of his mind. The same chaplain also
observed that Catholics had fought in all previous wars
and never failed to kill their share of the enemy. "There
are priests and priests," Downey said. "Several months
after I'd been at Jackson, I was in New York on a short
leave and talked with a priest at the Catholic Peace
Fellowship offices. He counselled me to believe in my
conscience."

   In due course, Downey continued, he received orders
to ship out from Jackson as a member of an artillery
division. When the day of departure came, Downey and
others assembled before parked buses that were to take

them to an airport. Routinely checking attendance as the
men boarded, a first sergeant called out each man's name,
but when Downey's turn came he refused to enter a bus.
The next thing he knew, he was standing at attention
before the brigade commander, a colonel, who irately
asked Downey what he intended doing. "Sir," he replied,
"the question is what are *you* going to do?" For an
answer, the colonel had an aide march Downey to the
Jackson stockade. According to Downey, the colonel told
the aide, "Put him in for six months. If he doesn't obey
his orders after that, give him another six months."
Downey had been in jail a week when a new chaplain
came into his life, a Baptist, who was making his pastoral
rounds of the stockade, benignly listening to the
complaints of those who had fallen from military grace.
Downey had no complaints. "I told him I was happy in
the stockade," Downey said. "I could avoid trouble in
there —I think that's all I tried to do for as long as I was in
the Army." After hearing Downey's story, the chaplain
had declared that Downey didn't belong in jail. The Army
had forms for conscientious objection, the chaplain said,
and he would be glad to help Downey fill them out. The
chaplain inquired whether Downey would be willing to
work in an Army hospital. Downey said yes. And would
Downey be willing to do so in Vietnam? Downey said
yes. The chaplain then relayed this information to the
brigade commander, who released Downey forthwith.

Over the next three weeks, Downey told me, the
chaplain helped him complete the forms, which first had
to go through channels at Jackson before submission to
the Pentagon for final disposition. Downey's company
commander, a tough airborne Ranger, was unsympathetic
to Downey's application but permitted him to see the
battalion's executive officer, a major, who was a West
Pointer and a Vietnam veteran. "I could sense his respect
at once," Downey said. "He knew from my record I
hadn't ever got out of line, except on trying to see this one
thing through." During their talk, the major, who was a

convert to Catholicism, asked Downey what he thought of Cardinal Spellman's endorsement of America's war policy in 1965, when the prelate said in Saigon, "My country, may it always be right. Right or wrong, my country," Downey replied, "I consider that immoral." From the major, he was sent on to a colonel, who had impressed the enlisted man. "He let me know he had a son who felt about violence exactly as I did," Downey told me. The papers were approved for submission to Washington, and Downey settled down to await their return in a capacity that spared him from handling weapons—he was made a typist-clerk at brigade head-quarters. In six months, the papers came back from Washington. They were disapproved. Downey told me, "I went to the captain and said, 'Send me back to the stockade.' His attitude toward me had changed, and all he said was 'I'm just a captain. I'm going to talk to the major.'"

For a while, it looked as though the officers' friendly auspices would save Downey, for, smoothly and efficient-ly, he found himself shifted from brigade headquarters to a specialists' school for typists, where a two months' training course was about to begin. The shift took place just as the company to which Downey had been assigned was being dispersed from Jackson. "Fortunately for my peace of mind, the fellows weren't sent to Asia," he said. Suddenly, though, as Downey was completing his course, the officers' plot failed. A levy for Vietnam troops came down, Downey told me, and he was among those chosen. The captain had tried to retain Downey in his own command, but it was no use. Neither he nor the major nor the colonel could any longer exert influence in behalf of Downey's conscientious objection. Power over that had passed into the hands of a master sergeant, a product of eighteen years' military service. He was the managerial factotum in the Military Police division that had direct charge of selecting the troops for Vietnam. "His name was Kennedy," Downey said. "Somone told him about me, and I heard him say, 'This guy's going to kill or be killed.' "

Downey resolved at once to go to Sweden; he had three weeks' leave in which to organize his family's departure. He had small appetite for it, particularly since his father wasn't well. (He died a week after his son arrived in Sweden.) "I hated turning my back on my country," Downey told me. "Naturally, here in Uppsala, it's making ends meet that's on my mind, but I won't soon forget that I had to break a contract. I've become more political than I used to be. The way I see it now, I may have taken a step against economic imperialism. Gandhi's revolution inspires me, but all this talk of violent revolution in America bothers me. It's playing into the hands of atheistic elements."

A few days before I left Sweden, I tried to have a look at the American Deserters Committee, the would-be political hub of the deserters' colony. I got in touch with Vincent A. Strollo, of whom Mrs. Nystrom had spoken warmly as one of her most willing helpers inside the A.D.C. A stockily built young man from the Philadelphia area, Strollo told me he had quit LaSalle College as a freshman, in 1966, when his father, a postal employee, had fallen ill. Determined to contribute to the family's support, Strollo, then nineteen, saw an Army recruiter, who assured him that if he volunteered for four years three of them would be spent in Germany, and that when he got out the G.I. Bill would enable him to go back to school. The deal was made, and Strollo had eventually settled down to a safe, quiet existence in Germany as a hospital clerk. It eroded his sense of self-regard, however, Strollo told me. At Landshut, and later at Ramstein, he saw officers and master sergeants engage in shady transactions, including the sale of Army trucks to German civilians. When G.I.s raised questions concerning America's policy in Vietnam, sergeants had encouraged other soldiers to haze them. Sounding the same note other deserters had, Strollo said, "When I enlisted, I had this idea there must be something idealistic to military life, that someone—maybe a general—was making valid decisions, but all I could hear in Germany was lifers talking about rackets."

In November, 1967, the flight of the Intrepid Four to Sweden made desertion a widespread topic of conversation. Several months later, a friend said to Strollo, "Let's go to Sweden tonight." "It was all I needed," Strollo told me. "I didn't want to waste two more years of my life. I didn't take my stereo equipment—just some records." The two left in Strollo's Volkswagen, and they slept in it their first nights in Stockholm. Their third or fourth day, a deserter sitting on a park bench heard Strollo and his friend speaking English, and two newcomers were added to the colony. Strollo's friend subtracted himself at the end of a week, returning to Germany, but Strollo remained, falling in at once with the A.D.C. He spoke of it gratefully. It had not only helped him find his first lodging, he said, but, far more important, given him an ideological grasp of world events that lent significance to his desertion. "I now realize that the U.S. has always been an imperialist force," he said. "The U.S. does not plan indoctrination of its people, but just the same that's what happens. Had I become a teacher back home, as I hoped, I would have been helping the system. The time has come for power to be distributed to the people. I am trying to improve America as a society." He had recited it all like a catechism, and I asked him if some of the words he had used weren't rather sweeping. "I never used them before I came to Sweden," he said good-naturedly. "Incidentally, I forgot to mention that Sweden is no better than the United States." He had a girl, and a job with an electronics firm, and he took science courses, but it was the A.D.C. that gave shape to everything. He wanted to tell me about the A.D.C., but he thought it would be more appropriate if I talked with the organization's leader and theoretician, a deserter by the name of Bill Jones. Strollo arranged for me to meet Jones the following day at the A.D.C. headquarters.

Jones didn't show. I waited for him forty minutes in the headquarters, a damp, dishevelled basement where a shaft of gray light filtered downward through the iron bars of a small window. Two deserters were present, neither of whom knew whether Jones would appear. Batting the breeze, one of them, lately a Navy carpenter, said that without physical exercise he tended to feel tense; he thought he had better find himself stevedore's work. Looking up at the window grille, his companion speculated on the possibility of "a right-wing tourist" tossing a bomb into the A.D.C.'s basement. Just as I was leaving, a short, pink-cheeked young man entered, greeted the others, and took two letters from a table. He joined me as I climbed the basement stairs, and asked me who I was. After I told him, he said, "I don't like the A.D.C. It's just where I pick up my mail." He was a deserter from upstate New York; he declined to give his name, saying that his desertion had caused his parents harassment from their neighbors. When we got out into the street, it was raining. He asked me to buy him something to eat, and we went into a nearby restaurant. "I'm not a political person," he said after he had eaten. "When I first got here, it was the A.D.C. that answered my questions. My head was full of them. Was it safe here? Did the C.I.A. tap your phone? How did you meet girls? Where could you get *Mad* magazine?" Politically, though, the A.D.C. wasn't much use, as he saw it. Its leaders, he claimed, pushed a single view, and while his own politics were vague, he was dead set against "sameness," no matter what its form. Maybe the Army had done that to him, he conjectured. "It was a prison of sameness," he said. He watched the rain fall against the restaurant window. "This weather is when I like Stockholm best," he said. "I know its places now—the

Strandvägen, the NK store, the T-Centralen. If I had
enough money to call home a dozen times a year, I might
be satisfied, by which I don't mean that I'm ready to settle
down here, or anywhere else. I don't even want a job. In
fact, all I feel like doing is taking off for Prague. Still,
those dozen calls would be nice. The U.S. is a part of my
life, but so is being young, and for a rotten war like this it
just isn't worth forgetting the things that can go with
being young."

That evening, I phoned Strollo, who, apologetically,
arranged a second appointment for me with Jones.
"Tomorrow afternoon at four at the pad," Strollo said,
referring to an apartment the A.D.C. maintained at
Karlbergsvägen 52. Strollo also told me that Jones had
said he would have on hand some tapes of radio
broadcasts that he and other members of the A.D.C. had
made for the Vietcong and Hanoi; U.S. troops in Vietnam
listened to the broadcasts, and I had expressed an interest
in hearing them.

Jones was present the following day. A tall, good-look-
ing man, he had deserted from Germany; prior to entering
the Army, he had studied for the priesthood at Loyola
University, in Chicago. Our meeting was a fiasco. His
opening words to me were "I hear you talked to those two
fellows at our headquarters yesterday." He fixed me with
a sullen, suspicious expression. He was seated at the
center of a circle of several adherents, who, it appeared,
had gathered to watch him take me on. There were others
elsewhere in the apartment, a dim, rambling dormitory of
six or seven rooms, where deserters, homeless or
otherwise, could come in off the streets. I asked Jones his
conception of the A.D.C.'s purpose, and he answered that
desertion by itself "might degenerate into a Boy Scout
thing" unless it was validated by political action. He was
momentarily interrupted when Strollo arrived, adding
himself to the group near Jones. Continuing, Jones
volunteered the information that Students for a Demo-
cratic Society had conferred chapter status on the A.D.C.

When I inquired whether he favored any particular faction in the S.D.S., he said, "The S.D.S.'s recognition legitimizes us as part of an *American* movement." The A.D.C. was doing its best to promote that movement, he declared, citing the fact that the A.D.C. was regularly circulating its publication, *Second Front,* among thousands of United States troops. In addition, he said, there were the broadcasts that he and Strollo and others made for Hanoi and the National Liberation Front; both had delegations in Stockholm, and their representatives had said the A.D.C. broadcasts were popular with G.I.s in Vietnam.

Genially, Strollo put in, "We usually start the broadcasts with a little rock—Jimi Hendrix, Moby Grape, groups like that."

Jones considered it "patriotic" to broadcast for Hanoi and the Vietcong. "It's helping G.I.s," he said.

I asked whether I could hear one or two of the tapes, and Jones said he had none. I glanced at Strollo, who looked unhappy. When I told Jones I had been promised I would be able to hear the tapes, he sat silent, his expression as sullen as when I arrived.

I moved toward the door, and Strollo walked with me part of the way, mumbling something to the effect that Jones had been burned by previous interviewers. Anyway, I said, trying to make the best of matters, Jones had inadvertently reminded me that Hanoi and the Vietcong had delegations in Sweden. Remarking that perhaps I should avail myself of a chance to talk with them, I asked Strollo whether he could facilitate my meeting a Vietcong representative.

He shook his head. Half turning toward Jones, he replied, "You might write something about them. We don't know what you would write."

The Vietcong offices in Stockholm were a collection of several sparsely furnished cubicles on the third floor of a shabby building at Drottninggatan 13. I was granted an interview there with a short, serious man with graying

hair named Le Phuong, who was an official of the
Provisional Revolutionary Government, the Vietcong's
diplomatic title. American troops were deserting in
Vietnam, Le Phuong told me; he had no exact figures, but
the rate of desertion had gone up since President Nixon
had first talked of a pullout. There were deserters in
Saigon itself, he said—G.I.s who had put on mufti and
melted into the white civilian population of Greek
businessmen, French journalists, and other foreigners. Le
Phuong didn't want me to think, however, that Americans
were deserting in anything like the numbers in which the
French had toward the end of their long reign in Vietnam.
They would come over in droves, waving white handker-
chiefs, he recalled, adding, "We had strict orders not to
shoot. Anyone who did was sent to jail." The same policy
was in force again, Le Phuong told me; the National
Liberation Front's radio continually emphasized that fact
to American units, and the voices of the N.L.F.
announcers were often those of deserters. That was about
the most use to which the Vietcong hoped to put
deserters. It was unreasonable to expect them to bear
arms, Le Phuong said. That would mean shooting at
fellow-Americans, and, besides, they were weary of the
war. They wanted to get out of Vietnam, he said, and the
N.L.F. helped them do so by setting them on their way to
Sweden and other havens. He handed me a blue
propaganda flyer, the text of which was attributed to a
black deserter who inveighed against "racism," "oppres-
sion," "imperialism."

From the clutter on his desk, Le Phuong produced
another exhibit—an unmailed letter, allegedly found on a
battlefield, in which a G.I. described his discontent to a
friend back home in Hadley, Massachusetts. I also
noticed on the desk a copy of an underground newspaper
from Berkeley, California, whose front page proclaimed
that "the American people" were in a state of high revolt
against the war. Tapping the newspaper, Le Phuong
seemed about to thrust it at me, but he didn't. He shut his

eyes a moment, and then announced in a determined
monotone, "I wish to say something." Gesturing toward
the newspaper, he said that in his mind he honored
America's "peace forces" but that their effect on the
American public did not appear to be decisive. Looking at
me directly, he said, "Your people judge the war by the
safety of their sons, not by the deaths of us Vietnamese.
We must go on killing your sons—as many of them as we
possibly can."

The last deserter I saw was Raymond Sansivero, a
compact young man with black hair. Like several of the
others, he had seen action as a Marine in Vietnam.
Sansivero's father was a taxi-driver in Huntington, Long
Island, and his mother worked for a medical-insurance
organization. He was barely out of high school when he
enlisted, in 1968, at the age of eighteen. Six months later,
he lay in a U.S. military hospital in Osaka, Japan,
wounded in his left leg and eye, the vision in which had
remained impaired. He had been hit at Khe Sanh. "I was
one of the lucky ones," he said. "A new corporal called in
the wrong coordinates, and our artillery got ten of
us—four killed." Sansivero told me of these and other
matters in his one-room apartment, with kitchenette, on
the fifth floor of a walkup in a nondescript Stockholm
district. We sat on the household's bed—a mattress on the
floor. The room was close and still. Sansivero's two-
month-old son lay asleep in a crib, and the infant's
mother, Maria, a short, worried Swedish girl, hovered
nearby. "The baby's got fever," Sansivero said, speaking
low as he glanced anxiously at his wife. Occupying the
one chair in the room was a new deserter—a high-school
friend of Sansivero's. He was spending his second day in
Sweden, and, staring down at Sansivero and me half
recumbent on the mattress, he followed the interview
with curiosity, as though he imagined it was a ritual to
which all deserters submitted.

For Sansivero, I gathered, joining the Marines had been the equivalent of enrolling in a vocational school. He had had no idea what the war was about, he told me, but he was unable to afford college and he knew he had to learn a trade. Another thing he knew was that the Marines ran a school for aviation mechanics, and that, he figured, was for him, even though it meant signing up for four years. Once in uniform, he took a flock of physical and aptitude tests, one of which had disclosed that he was color-blind. As a result, his ambition to become an aviation mechanic went out the window. "I was put in the infantry," Sansivero said. "I didn't mind. I'd often heard my parents say that we were all obligated to do our bit for our country."

After he completed basic training, he was flown to Danang, where he was struck by the animosities that existed between officers and enlisted men. There was tension even at Khe Sanh, the besieged valley where his combat experiences were largely concentrated. "We took thirteen hundred rockets there one day," he recalled. "We tried to stay underground, but we had to go out and get food and ammunition. Those were the last errands some of the guys ever ran." In Sansivero's opinion, the South Vietnamese troops at Khe Sanh were practically use-less—undisciplined, demoralized, and so filthy in their habits that they had attracted rats. But it was the South Vietnamese civilians who had made the most profound impression on him. "They didn't like us, and we didn't like them back for it," he told me. "When we came near one of their hamlets, they would disappear inside their homes. They never gave us information, so we'd round up some of them and ship them off to Danang for questioning. There was no use kidding ourselves. We got their message. Those people had no love or respect for us. I realized someone big in Washington had made a mistake but he was too proud to correct it. I realized I wasn't fighting for freedom or for any of the other things I

had been taught at Huntington High School." The new
deserter nodded vigorously.

While Sansivero was hospitalized in Japan, his morale
was further lowered when a sergeant ordered him to clean
toilets. Sansivero refused, and the sergeant took to
marking him absent whenever he left his bed. One day, a
Marine colonel came to his bed and presented him with
some ribbons, including a Purple Heart and a Presidential Unit Citation. The following day, the same colonel,
responding to the sergeant's reports, demoted Sansivero
from E-3 to private. When Sansivero protested, the
colonel said, "My N.C.O.s don't lie." Glancing over at his
child as it stirred feverishly in its crib, Sansivero said,
"One day ribbons, the next day busted. I was well enough
to split, so that's what I did." He drew a thousand dollars
in back pay and left for Tokyo. His first afternoon there,
he met a Japanese girl who turned out to be a member of
the Zengakuren, a militant leftist group that encouraged
desertion. Yielding to the Japanese girl's persuasion, he
went to the northern island of Hokkaido, off the Russian
coast, where, Sansivero told me, a Soviet gunboat had
called for him and two other deserters—another Marine,
by the name of Randy Coates, and You Tsi Oyang, an
Army sergeant from Manhattan. "It was all out of a
storybook," Sansivero told me. "My first champagne and
caviar. There were two interpreters aboard—mean-look-
ing Russians who were probably enforcers. They had
pointy shoes and raincoats down to here. They said to call
them Mike and Stanley. They said they'd take care of us,
that our worries were over. They also said that when we
got to Moscow we were to steer clear of American
correspondents, that there'd be Russian ones for us to talk
to."

Sansivero spent two months in Russia, where, by his
teen-ager's standards, he was shown a wonderful time.
He brought me some souvenirs from a wooden shelf on
the wall above where his high-school friend was sitting,
and I glanced at the titles of several Marxist-Leninist

tracts and the snapshot of a Russian girl. "That's Luba,"
Sansivero said, as his high-school friend snatched the
mementos from me. In Moscow, Sansivero went on, he
and the other deserters had stayed for three weeks in a
penthouse at the Hotel Sputnik. "Caviar and tomatoes for
breakfast," he recalled. They had passed other pleasant
weeks at a country place outside Moscow that had an
enormous garden and floodlights for night parties. In
mid-July, the adventure ended when a Soviet function-
ary, presenting the deserters with the Marxist-Leninist
tracts, told them, "Read these, and then go home and
make your country better." The Russians arranged to fly
the deserters to Stockholm, and at the Moscow airport the
young Americans were ushered into a special waiting
room for V.I.P.s, from which the press was barred. When
the plane was ready for boarding, two military guards
escorted the G.I.s to first-class seats before the other
passengers were permitted to get on. "We had on black
Russian suits," Sansivero said. "Everyone thought we
were big-shot Communists. I remember American tourists walking past our seats real slow to get a good look at
us."

In Sweden, the three deserters separated. Sansivero was
uncertain what had become of Oyang; Coates had turned
himself in at the American Embassy. Sansivero said that
he himself had tried to do that the previous summer. "I
thought that if maybe I could be promised a light
sentence, I'd get everything over and done with," he said.
However, the Embassy official he saw had no authority to
offer specific terms, and Sansivero was not willing to take
chances. An Army deserter in need of psychiatric
attention had recently done that and been sentenced to
four years at hard labor. Sansivero believed that he would
be punished even more severely, since he had enabled the
Russians to make propaganda capital of his desertion. "I
didn't think I could take the brig for too long—I'd heard
so many stories about it," he said. Unlike other deserters,
Sansivero said he would go back like a shot if the

government offered amnesty. "If you have it on the ball, you can make it in America," he told me. "A few things need to be changed there, like foreign policy and race, but there's nothing wrong with the free-enterprise system." Thwarted at the Embassy, he had settled down to trying to make it in Sweden. Some things had gone right, he said. There was Maria, and the baby; his parents were coming over in a few months to meet them. He was planning to attend a Swedish vocational school. For a while, he said, he had been active in behalf of the A.D.C., but the day I saw him he was fed up with that organization in particular and politics in general. "I want to be left alone," he said. "I want to finish my education and get a job and be a human being. It's up to the government people who goofed us into the war to get us out of it. I'd fight again if someone attacked the U.S., or even if the Chinese went into Vietnam, but one thing I know is that I'm not going to kill anyone for anyone, not without there being a damn good reason for it."

After I got back to America, I read in a newspaper that Sansivero had ceased trying to make it in Sweden. Overcoming his fear of the brig, he had given himself up at the United States Embassy, which had paid his fare to Kennedy Airport, where he was arrested upon landing. Maria and the baby had preceded the Marine by a few days, their fare having been paid by his parents. Sansivero was flown to Camp Lejeune, North Carolina, charged with desertion. His court-martial had yet to take place. Until it did, and perhaps for a long time afterward, he would remain in the brig.

3

HOME AGAIN, 1971

🏴 🏴 🏴 🏴 🏴

Deserters weren't the only young Americans out of uniform while their country was at war. Honorably discharged servicemen were also in mufti, for by 1971, two years before the United States agreed to pull out of Indo-China, two and a half million new veterans were pursuing civilian lives—unarmed bystanders as the war continued. Frank Reed, as I shall call him, was among these new veterans and, like most of them, he concentrated hard in this unresolved period on putting together a career. A twenty-six-year-old former sergeant in the Marine Corps who had seen considerable combat, Reed had found work as an apprentice salesman for a giant internationally famous firm, the United Metals Company of America (also a pseudonym). He reported daily to its Manhattan headquarters, high in the Chrysler Building, where he shared a large open office with scores of fellow-employees in the sales division, each of whom had a desk and a telephone; several of the desks near Reed's bore small American flags. Reed liked his work,

but, not surprisingly, he found, he said, that it had its
don'ts. "I can't wear slacks to the office and I can't talk
about the war with customers," he said. There were times
when he found the latter restriction especially trying. It
cost him an effort, he told me, to listen in respectful
silence while a senior executive, chatting before the
opening of a sales conference, held forth approvingly on
America's intervention in Asia. Fortunately, this sort of
thing didn't happen often, and when it did the executives
were unaware they were addressing a combat veteran of
the Vietnam war. "It's just as well they don't know," Reed
said. "They'd ask me my opinion of the fighting, and I'd
have to answer that there isn't a veteran I know, including
myself, who has come back all charged up about the war.
At this point in my career, I don't care to get into any
hassles with executives. I want to make it here. Call me
straight. Plenty of my veteran friends do. They bug me for
saying our system still has a chance. But I know I'm not
nearly as straight as I used to be. Before I was in the
Marines, I used to dream of becoming a big-shot
corporation exec, like my father. I still have a hankering
for that, but combat in Vietnam has made changes in my
thinking. Maybe they won't last, but for now they have
me imagining I'm leading two lives."

Reed and I discussed his reflections on the unfinished
war at some length, taking them up at his home; at a
military hospital in downtown Manhattan, where he was
visiting a wounded friend of his; and at the offices of a
veterans' organization he belonged to, where I met
several other friends of his. Most of our time together was
spent at his three-room apartment in a high-rise housing
complex on the upper West Side. Listening to Reed, I had
the impression that many of the changes in his thinking,
as he called them, were highly tentative; they seemed
more like questions with which he was still wrestling.
Another impression he gave me was that eventually he
might succeed in unifying his two lives. In large part, this
impression derived from his physical bearing. He was a

big, husky, outgoing man with a hearty voice—attributes
that lent him a general aura of confidence. His hair was
reddish, and his sideburns primly short, in keeping with
company policy. He had small blue eyes and a scarred
chin, from a boyhood accident in Louisville, Kentucky,
where he was born. Occasionally, as we talked, his eyes
betrayed a flicker of uncertainty, and once or twice of
sharp regret. In all other respects, however, he seemed an
almost rambunctiously physical being, often moving
about his rectangular living room with a buoyant, athletic
energy. He did this even though he was limping when we
met; a knee injury he had suffered as a high-school
football player had been acting up. Now and then, in
telling me about himself, Reed casually referred to
fistfights he had had; in describing a Marine friend who
was killed near the Demilitarized Zone, he said, "We got
to be buddies after he jumped me in a bar." Even the
walls of Reed's living room attested to his physical
disposition, for hanging on their white expanse were
three fraternity paddles—broad Greek-lettered bats of the
kind used at initiation ceremonies. The paddles, he told
me, were mementos of his days at the University of
Tennessee, in Knoxville; his father, a successful steel
executive in Pittsburgh, was also an alumnus of Tennessee. Idly reading off the Greek letters on the paddles,
Reed added, "A racist fraternity if there ever was one, and
I knew it when I pledged." He had scarcely spoken when
a black man of about thirty, slender and mustached,
walked into the living room from the kitchenette. Reed
introduced him as his roommate, Emerson Hayes. (His
name, like all others here, has been changed.) It was a
Sunday morning, but Hayes was on his way to work. He
was a guidance counsellor for the New York City Board of
Education. As the roommates eyed each other appraising-
ly, Reed said, "Em's job turns him on. He's at it seven
days a week." When Reed and I were alone again, he told
me that he had met Hayes in the sales division of United
Metals, from which Hayes had recently resigned to take

the school job. They had been sharing the apartment for five months. "I found the place; Em had the furniture," Reed said. "It's worked out, I think, but we've never become close." He looked disappointed for a moment, then told me that Hayes would be moving out in two weeks. Reed pointed in the direction of an unpainted bookcase, atop which rested a large photograph of a blond girl. "That's Lucy," he said. "We'll be married next month down in Knoxville, in her church. She's Catholic, I'm Presbyterian. After that, we'll live here." They had known each other as students at the University of Tennessee, from which Lucy was about to graduate. Reed spoke proudly of her. A week earlier, she had made her first visit to New York and found herself a job at Altman's; she already had all sorts of ideas for redecorating the apartment. He gazed at her photograph. "Lucy says to forget the war," he told me. "She says it doesn't affect me anymore—that I've done my bit."

Reed was eighteen when he enlisted in the Marines for four years. He did it, he told me, because he had done poorly at high school, in Cedarville, Pennsylvania, which is a fashionable suburb of Pittsburgh; Reed's parents and a younger brother and sister still lived there. Except for math, in which he was strong, he was constantly on the verge of flunking all his courses. It was not until a certain week in the spring of his senior year, however, that his fortunes, academic and otherwise, hit rock bottom. The week featured three disasters, the first of which involved a girl classmate who accused Reed of having made her pregnant. Two days later, she changed her mind. "Dad thought the whole thing was funny. Mother didn't," Reed told me. The week's second incident took place when Reed borrowed the family car and, coaxed by a couple of pals, entered it in a drag race—a step that entailed, among other things, pulling off the tires, putting on drag slicks, and tuning up the engine. Reed won, but when news of the victory reached home his father hit the ceiling.

"Mother thought that it was funny," Reed said. The climax of the week came when Reed, walking down a school corridor between classes, heard a commotion inside the boys' lavatory. Investigating, he found several classmates beating up one of his friends. When Reed asked what was going on, three of the attacking group went for him. After peeling off two of them, he was rhythmically belting the third when a teacher arrived. Reed was suspended for three days, and an immediate consequence was a solemn declaration by his father and mother that under no circumstances would they ever send him to college. Disheartened, Reed foresaw a future of pumping gas. It was then that he decided to enlist in the Marines for four years. It seemed a master stroke for restoring himself to the human race; his parents heartily agreed.

That summer, Reed took basic training at Camp Lejeune, North Carolina. It was 1963, well before the United States committed large forces to the fighting in Vietnam, and his life in the Marines, he told me, proceeded agreeably. He liked the camaraderie, and he also liked the travel. Aboard Navy ships, he cruised the Caribbean and, in 1964, the Mediterranean, where his vessel put in at a small Turkish port, among other places. "Tegekac," Reed said, carefully identifying it. He and his detachment went ashore there for a day of military maneuvers, Reed related, after which, toward twilight, the men, weary but exhilarated, straggled back to the landing beach to await the boats that would return them to their troopship. On the beach, Reed continued, nothing much occurred until, suddenly, a huge turtle emerged from bulrushes near the water's edge. In no time, Reed said, two Marines had poured lighter fluid on the reptile and set it afire. But the fire didn't catch, and a couple of other men, encircled by fascinated comrades, including Reed, added gasoline. The turtle tried to escape, Reed said, fitfully inching itself along some hopeless route. In an hour, Reed said, its blistering, melting shell had

moved no more than ten feet. "It was still burning when
our boats picked us up," Reed told me. "During the ride
out, I wondered how it was possible for guys to be that
inhumane. It bothered me that I hadn't said anything. I
had nightmares about the turtle. In Vietnam, the times I
was shook up worst were when I knew for sure that our
weapons were burning people."

Reed and his outfit, part of the First Marine Amphibi-
ous Brigade, which consisted of nearly four thousand
men, were in Hawaii when they were ordered to Vietnam.
It was July, 1965, and the big American buildup was
under way. Reed estimated that when he reached Vietnam
there were seventy thousand Americans there; when he
left, thirteen months later, the number had quadrupled
and troops were continuing to pour in. Sailing from
Hawaii, Reed recalled, he held but a single conviction
about the war: he wished it were being fought in a place
with a less sultry climate. "Hot weather affects my skin,"
he said. Certainly, Reed went on, he had never reflected
on whether his impending combat had political or moral
implications. In that connection, Reed said, he knew only
the catechism that all Marines were taught. Summarizing
it, he said, "If South Vietnam fell, that would be the end
of Asia, and Communism would take over everywhere.
We were the good guys, they were the bad guys."

Reed's unit landed at Danang, then moved on up to
Chu Lai, a coastal town, where the First Brigade had set
up a base of operations. From it, Reed and other Marines
fared forth on frequent patrols, but at this point the
enemy was lying low. Bored, the men developed an itch
for heroics. In six weeks, they had all the action they
craved. It came in the form of Operation Starlight, a drive
against the First North Vietnamese Regiment, which was
deployed six miles south of Chu Lai. Reed's duties were
those of a forward artillery observer; as part of advancing
American elements, he called in rounds of fire and
corrected trajectories. On the first day of Starlight, half of
Reed's company of two hundred men were killed or

wounded. Two hours after the operation started, a lieutenant leading Reed's platoon was killed, and Reed took his place, for which he was later given a combat meritorious promotion to corporal. Reed's principal memory of the gruelling week, though, concerns the night following its fourth day. At that time, he and his men were permitted to leave their forward positions to sleep a few hours at an artillery base that was theoretically well protected by Marine guards, barbed-wire fences, and mines; periodically, flares illuminated the sky to expose trespassers. It turned out that these precautions weren't enough. At one in the morning, Reed, alone and unarmed, was crossing a field to rejoin his platoon after leaving a latrine when an exploding flare revealed a North Vietnamese soldier a hundred feet ahead. The man was holding a machine gun, its barrel aimed at Reed. For an instant, the two stared at each other, and then the infiltrator shot. Reed threw himself to the ground, but the infiltrator didn't—something that puzzled Reed long after. The field was littered with automatic rifles, and Reed, crawling a few feet to where one of them lay, grabbed it and returned the fire. His first burst was high, but seconds later he hit his standing target repeatedly. Reed now shouted a warning of infiltrators, and fresh flares were set off. A Marine sweep of the perimeter was organized, but Reed stayed where he was, his gaze fixed on his victim, brilliantly visible in the synthetic daylight. "It's rare to see someone you kill in combat," Reed told me. "The North Vietnamese soldier and I had faced each other, and seeing him now, curled up out there, details came back to me. He seemed older than I was, and tall for a Vietnamese. It sounds crazy, considering what he was trying to do to me, but I started thinking that in a different time and place he and I might have been friends. Why should we have tried to kill each other? The rifle was still in my hands, and I threw it aside. Maybe he had been a husband and father. Maybe I had killed a man who was going to be a great doctor. I tried to stop thinking about

him, but the only other thought that came to me didn't
help. What about all those times I'd directed artillery fire?
It suddenly struck me that there might be plenty of
unseen people I'd killed."

After his duel with the infiltrator, Reed went on, he
grew conscious of the Vietnamese as individuals; until
then, he said, he had thought of them as a conglomerate
mass. It was difficult to indulge his new curiosity,
however. For one thing, there were Vietnamese he was
busy fighting, and, for another, officers discouraged
conversation with all natives—that is, those who could
manage pidgin English. After Starlight, Reed said, he also
began to puzzle over what it was that enabled North
Vietnamese regulars and Vietcong to stand up to superior
American firepower. They had no air force, navy,
helicopters, or tanks, and, as often as not, Vietcong
guerrillas at that time carried rifles that had to be reloaded
after each shot. "We were fighting underdogs," Reed said.
"All they had was their own country, and we were in it."
It was a beautiful country, he added, as anyone could tell
by the frequency with which Marines took out their
cameras at sunset when iridescent pinks and greens
outlined the lush landscape. His own favorite place, Reed
said, was an immense beach near Chu Lai, whose waters
were pearly and clear, and where he and other Marines
liked to swim in the nude. Village women used a nearby
bay for laundering. The women, he told me, were a
quarter of a mile from where the men swam, and
sometimes, yielding to an impulse, the Marines, in a pack,
would jog toward the women, yahooing, and then dance
around them, aware that Buddhism, the women's
religion, forbade them to look upon naked men. "In
Vietnam, I didn't think about that twice," Reed said. "It
was just something we were entitled to, like having Bob
Hope for entertainment."

The country was as impoverished as it was beautiful,
Reed continued, with its inhabitants prepared to put in a
hard day's work for, literally, slops. "We had native

servants we paid in food leftovers," Reed said. "We'd
stand around and watch the Vietnamese scavenge our
garbage cans, grabbing what they could for themselves
and their pigs." The Vietnamese, he said, would do
anything for food. Once, he recalled, when he and a
squad in his charge were being transported by truck to a
new position, there was a brief halt in a village near Phu
Bai. Immediately, swarms of townspeople surrounded
the vehicle, begging the Marines for food. Some of the
men tossed out candies, but one, winding up like a
baseball pitcher, hurled a can of C rations at a small boy,
who fell to the ground with blood streaming from his
temple. The Vietnamese moved to the boy's side, and the
transport driver stepped on the accelerator. Reed said, "I
should have chewed out the Marine, but I didn't. I
figured he'd done one of those things that guys do in a
war."

In only a single instance, Reed told me, did he succeed
in feeling moderately close to a Vietnamese, and that was
but a fleeting experience. Late in November, 1965, he
said, he and a friend, a Marine captain, left their artillery
base in a jeep to drive to a cafe in An Tan, a hamlet three
miles away, where the captain liked to have a beer. Reed
himself had never been to the cafe, which, as the captain
mentioned in the jeep, was run by a family of husband,
wife, and son, all of whom spoke English. The cafe
turned out to be little more than a bamboo shack with five
metal tables; from them one could look on An Tan's main
street—a few houses and souvenir shops, some native
pedestrians, and an occasional oxcart. Reed and the
captain were the only patrons. When they had been ten
minutes over their beers, a young boy—the proprietor's
son—entered from the rear of the cafe and, sitting down at
one of the tables, buried himself in a book. Curious, Reed
walked over to see what he was reading. It was a math
book, Reed told me, and an astonishing one. "The boy
was into calculus," he said. "I recognized the integration
signs. He was studying math that was college level back

home." The boy's mother came over, and Reed learned
from her that her son was eleven. He congratulated her,
and she talked of other subjects that the boy was
studying—Vietnamese history, English, and French. On
the way back to the artillery base, Reed said, he felt
heartened by the thought of the boy's gifts. "They were
his and his alone," he said. "It made Vietnam seem less
strange to me."

Early one morning in December, 1965, Reed, acting as
a forward artillery observer, radioed his Fire Direction
Center, in the rear, to send over several rounds of smoke
shells to conceal advancing American troops. In short
order, he told me, shells did come over, but they behaved
oddly, falling in an erratic pattern, far beyond the target
area and into the vicinity of villages and hamlets. Reed
radioed again. "What are you guys shooting?" he asked.
"Willie Peter," a lieutenant replied. Reed gasped. "That's
not what I called for," he said. Willie Peter was the term
used for white phosphorus, a substance that created
smoke but was primarily intended for searing through the
armor of tanks and heavy guns; a pinch of the stuff
burned through a human hand. The firing stopped, but
Reed knew that unsuspecting victims must have been
burned. As he looked up at the insidious fog drifting
westward, he realized he was witnessing an accident, but
what, he asked himself, was he to make of it? "I said to
myself, 'My God, this war had better be for a wonderful,
idealistic reason,'" Reed told me. "It wasn't the one I'd
been taught. I'd seen enough of the Vietnamese to know
that. They could hack us up in their country, but that
didn't mean they were a threat to ours. It was the first time
I knew I had doubts about our policy, and it caught me by
surprise. I'd been raised to think the government was like
a church—something to have faith in, especially in time
of war."
Reed didn't share his doubts with his fellow-Marines.
At that time, he said, few troops admitted to doubts, even

if they had them. Harboring his own, as he did after that
morning, he found that the men in his unit suddenly
seemed strangers, like the Vietnamese. He fought and
lived with them, Reed said, but he didn't know whether
they believed in what they were doing. Of course, Reed
observed, he could have asked, but that might have
disturbed the surface contentment that prevailed in his
unit. There was no belittling that contentment. In part, he
told me, it was a survival technique: the more harmoni-
ously the men got along, the likelier they would be to save
each other in combat. Conversely, Reed went on, combat
itself inspired genuine affection among the men. He
himself had good friends, Reed said; he didn't want to
lose them, possibly, by airing his confusions over the
child mathematician, the Willie Peter shells, the food
slops. He mentioned a few of his friends. Two were
drinking companions, and they and Reed were known as
the Three Musketeers. Another was a West Virginian, the
company's best guitarist, who planned to study for the
priesthood after the war. Reed's most important friend
was Ralph Jackson III, a nineteen-year-old black corporal
from Pittsburgh, whose wife was expecting their second
child. He and Reed had been in boot camp together,
where they had often competed against each other at track
meets. Reed described Jackson as an artless, sunny man
whose manner had a curiously encouraging effect on
those around him; Marines would follow him to Sunday
services, he said, just to be near him. Jackson never used
drugs or foul language. "He was an All-American boy,"
Reed said. "Except for his color, he was everything my
parents wanted me to be."

The fighting increased steadily. Reacting to the
American buildup, Hanoi and the Vietcong grew more
and more adept at their type of warfare—ambushes,
sabotage, hit-and-run attacks. "They were on their soil,
and their morale was high," Reed said. As the pressure
mounted, he listened closely for intimations of doubt
among his comrades, but all he heard was the usual talk

about "round-eye" girls back home. "I was sure the guys
were holding things in. I couldn't believe I was all that
different from everyone else," he said. The Marines, Reed
told me, fought with determination and often with anger.
"When someone was blown away, his buddy would
volunteer for a patrol and start shooting the first chance
he had," he said. He saw no full-scale atrocities, he told
me, but even so it was possible to witness ugly events. On
Christmas Day, 1965, a thirty-hour truce was in effect, but
he was sent out on patrol; two of his men were killed. In
February, Reed became the last of the Three Musketeers.
The guitarist was killed shortly afterward. Another friend
stepped on a mine, losing his legs. Reed said, "A medic
ran to him with a tourniquet, and while he was applying
it my friend slipped the medic's .45 from its holster and
blew out his brains." Jackson died in May, 1966,
ambushed by the Vietcong, and Reed's doubts about
everything were intensified. He wrote Jackson's widow,
describing—inadequately, he said—her husband's influence on him.

The remainder of Reed's days in Vietnam were spent in
a succession of patrols, their dangerous monotony
relieved by the details of particular actions. In June, on a
dry, bright morning, Reed saw an enemy soldier at closer
range than he had seen the North Vietnamese infiltrator.
This occurred outside Tam Ky, a village where Marines
commanded by Reed, now a sergeant, routed a group of
Vietcong. Four were killed, four fled into a forest, and one
was caught by an eighteen-year-old Marine, newly
arrived in Vietnam, who recklessly chased the Vietcong.
Ordering his captive to raise his hands, the Marine urged
him on toward Reed and the rest of the patrol, a hundred
yards away. As the Vietcong, his hands held high,
approached the Marines, Reed peered at his features. "He
was definitely younger than the North Vietnamese
infiltrator," he told me. "He was also shorter, by maybe
four inches. He had on torn black pajamas, and he was
wearing what we called Jesus boots—sandals with soles

made of rubber tire and with rope crisscrossing the legs."
When the pair were twenty feet from the patrol, Reed's
second-in-command, a corporal, detached himself from
the others. "Stand aside!" he barked at the new Marine,
who obeyed. The next instant, the corporal sprayed the
Vietcong with a half-dozen rounds, their force spattering
some of the Marines with the guerrilla's blood. Enraged,
Reed reported the corporal to his superior, a gunnery
sergeant, as soon as the patrol reached camp. The gunnery
sergeant told him to shut up. Reed went to a major, who
said, "Whatever the gunny says, that's what goes." The
next day, Reed talked with a lieutenant colonel, who said,
"Be cool." Reed's zeal was gone. His voice fairly
grinding, he told me, "I ended up doing what the gunny
said—I shut up."

In July, 1966, it was all over. Chanting "We're Number
One," Reed and a contingent from his brigade took off
from Danang for the States. They stopped in Okinawa for
three hours. Reed said, "We were searched for dope, and
after that we were in the air again, bound for the land of
round-eyes."
Reed spent his first week in America in a naval hospital
at the El Toro Marine Corps Air Station, in California,
undergoing treatment for jungle rot, a fungus disease he
had contracted in Vietnam. Once he was released from
the hospital, an eternity of freedom beckoned—first,
several weeks' leave, after which he would finish his
Marine service safe in the United States. He had no plans
except to fly home to Cedarville. His family welcomed
him warmly—especially his ten-year-old brother, Petey,
who stared worshipfully at the returned hero, uniformed,
beribboned, erect. Reed was soon in mufti for his leave,
but that didn't diminish Petey's worship. "We'd always
liked each other a lot," Reed told me. Petey alone, in all
Cedarville, paid him homage, Reed said. Certainly the
girls didn't throw flowers at him, as he had once dreamed
they would. In the years since his enlistment, he

discovered, the war had become a source of concern to his
contemporaries. They spoke so anxiously of the draft, he
said, that he felt he should make little of the fact that he
had put Vietnam behind him. One of his friends, though,
made a great deal of the fact. He was a physically
handicapped young man named Joe Baird, the valedicto-
rian of Reed's high-school class, whom Reed had long
held in esteem. Their first evening together after Reed's
return, he startled the veteran by declaring that he had no
regrets at being unable to serve in a war like the Vietnam
war. We had no business in Indo-China, he asserted, and
he proceeded to set forth reasons for his view, all of them
news to Reed. President Eisenhower, Baird said, had
opposed the holding, in 1956, of a plebiscite that would
have enabled all Vietnamese, North and South, to
determine their own kind of government, since Ho Chi
Minh would have won any such plebiscite overwhelm-
ingly. In 1964, Baird continued, the United States
government had accused Hanoi of attacking its warships
in the Gulf of Tonkin—a charge that many American
public figures were openly suspicious of; the alleged
attack had led to the American troop buildup in Vietnam,
of which Reed himself had been a part. And at about the
time of the Tonkin incident, Baird stated, the United
States had brushed aside a North Vietnamese peace feeler
so palpable that the Secretary-General of the United
Nations, supposedly a neutral moderator, strongly criti-
cized the American action. Reed told me that when he
heard these points for the first time, in 1966, from Baird,
they confused and even angered him. "I didn't care to be
told that Starlight and the rest had been less than
nothing," he said. Baird's remarks, Reed told me, served
to deal a second blow to a surprising mood of optimism in
which he had come home. Once safe in Cedarville again,
he had decided that he faced a future alive with
possibilities, and that he would do best to forget the war.
The first blow had occurred on his second day home. At
ten o'clock that morning, Petcy, following his big

brother's instructions, had walked into Reed's bedroom and shaken him awake. In the grip of a nightmare, Reed had let out a yell and leaped at Petey's throat. The boy had wept uncontrollably, and Reed had been hours calming him down. That evening, alone with his parents after dinner, Reed told them that he knew for a fact he had killed a North Vietnamese soldier, and that it bothered him. "It wasn't your fault. Don't think about it," his mother advised him. His father changed the subject.

The summer weeks rolled by aimlessly, with Reed resuming old friendships, water-skiing on a town lake, and dating. The most important thing he did was to have a talk with his father about his future. He had been giving it a good deal of thought, he told his father, and had decided he would like to study business administration in college; specifically, Reed said, he was interested in the marketing end of salesmanship. His father replied that he had nothing against college as such, but he still didn't believe his son was college material. Reed was reminded of his dismal high-school record and of his parents' resolve to lay out no more money for his education. In short, his father concluded, Reed was free to attend school if he paid his own way. "I'm going to your college," Reed told his father. Alone in his room that night, thinking about the talk, Reed told me, he felt it incongruous that his high-school record should have figured so importantly in the conversation. It left him feeling, he said, that his year in Vietnam didn't count, that it might have been time spent at boarding school. Evidently, he said, his parents didn't realize that high school and combat were worlds apart. He was surprised that his father, who had served in the Navy in the Second World War, didn't realize it. In his room, Reed said, he found himself envying his father his war. It had had not only popular support but also definition and purpose. His father and the others had come home only after their mission was completed. The fighting in Vietnam had been going on before Reed got there, and still was raging. "It made being a civilian again seem unreal," he said.

Possibly because of this feeling, Reed said, he cut short his leave by two weeks and reported to Camp Lejeune for his final days as an active Marine. While he was there, he used the library facilities to do some research on Baird's assertions. He spent many hours poring over books and pamphlets, he said, and they generally bore out his friend's contentions. "There wasn't really much sense to the time I spent checking up on Joe Baird," he said. "What was the use of trying to find out why you had done something after it was done?"

In 1967, a few months after his discharge, Reed entered the College of Business Administration at the University of Tennessee, determined to prove that his attitude toward things academic had changed. He did so, earning his degree with high honors in three years. Moreover, he paid his own way, by means of G.I. benefits, savings from his time in the Marines, and scholarships he won. His chief satisfactions, though, he said, came from friends and from personal experiences. He met Lucy, the girl who was to become his fiancee, shortly after arriving in Knoxville. She was a local girl, and she often invited him to her home, where her family, a large one, treated him as if he were one of their own. Lucy's political outlook, to the extent that she claimed one, he told me, came from her father, a prominent lawyer who was active in American Legion affairs. Actually, Reed said, Lucy's views and her father's were the ones usually heard in Knoxville. Nearly everyone there, he said, including most students, assumed that the government, because it was the government, knew what it was doing abroad. Despite this atmosphere, Reed went on, he could tell, even amidst the distractions of his freshman year, that his concern over the war hadn't slackened. He told me he knew this when he felt impelled to write a letter to a Tennessee paper after it had printed an editorial questioning the patriotism of Americans who accused their military leaders of faking body counts of enemy dead. In his letter, Reed cited specific instances in which captured Vietcong, such as the one at Tam Ky, were killed in order to increase body counts; he also wrote that when a platoon or a company did report accurate body counts, higher echelons inflated them. His letter wasn't published.

In his sophomore year, Reed continued assiduously to prepare himself for a business career. He and Lucy were already planning to get married. He no longer had any illusions about forgetting the war. All sorts of incidents brought it sharply to mind. When Lucy's father took him to his Legion post for drinks one Sunday, Reed found himself put off by several Legionnaires who were especially delighted to learn he had seen combat. "Did you kill any gooks?" one Legionnaire asked.

When Reed nodded, another member of the post asked, "How many?"

Reed made up some wild number.

"How far from you were they?"

"It was all hand-to-hand," Reed replied.

"Did you use a knife?"

"No. I had a shovel—my lucky shovel."

At Lucy's urging, Reed told me, he joined his fraternity—one that enjoyed high prestige at Tennessee. The step, he said, turned out to be an important one, though for reasons that neither he nor Lucy anticipated. As a fraternity man, Reed lived in a house with a hundred and twenty-five "brothers," practically all of them, as Reed put it, "jocks and Wasps," from families of means, like his own. Reed was eventually elected vice-president of the chapter, and he told me that, on the whole, he enjoyed his two years in the house. There were many pleasant beer parties, he said, and he and his fraternity brothers often went on picnics in the nearby Great Smokies with sorority girls, Lucy among them. The talk at these get-togethers rarely touched on public issues, and that was just as well, Reed said, since everyone would have agreed on everything. There were times, though, when Reed felt himself out of step with the others, and, ruminating about it, he decided it had a lot to do with the fact that he was the only member of his chapter who had fought in Vietnam. Why else, he asked himself, would he recoil, as he did, on hearing his fraternity brothers speak of "niggers"? He was accustomed to hearing the term at home. Reed said—and, for that matter, on the Tennessee campus, where it was in fairly common use. But hearing it bandied about in the comfortable setting of his fraternity house recalled scenes near Chu Lai. He told me, "It was there that I first heard of dinks, slopes, and gooks. That was one of the places where we'd toss them slops to dive at." Memories of Ralph Jackson also made the term grate. Jackson was often on Reed's mind, and one evening late in 1969 when he had been thinking of his dead Marine friend he dropped into the fraternity lounge for a beer and some company. Joining four brothers, he listened to one of them tell a long joke in dialect about "niggers." When it was over, Reed heard himself say, "I knew blacks in Vietnam who were nice guys and good fighters." There was a silence, Reed said, until at last the storyteller, speaking patiently, told him, "Frank, there are colored people and there are niggers. In Vietnam, there are colored people only."

Reed told me that one of his fraternity brothers, an engineering student by the name of Ken Hanson, was an education in himself when the subject of the war came up. That was fairly often, Reed said, since Hanson, who was about to graduate, was obsessed with beating the draft. He was also obsessed with beating Hanoi. He wanted Haiphong mined and North Vietnam occupied. Hanson also considered it his patriotic duty to stay out of uniform. When Reed once asked him to explain this, Hanson replied, "A tenth-grader can handle a rifle, but someone like me has more important contributions to make. The kind of engineering job I could get, the government would be making a profit off me. I'd be

paying more in taxes than they'd have to pay me in the
armed forces." Reed had no doubt about Hanson's
sincerity. "I don't believe Ken was afraid of going to
Vietnam," Reed said. "He just didn't want his engineering career held up." Reed was impressed by the happy
ending to Hanson's campaign. Despite a high draft
number, which made it relatively unlikely that he would
be called, Hanson carefully limited his job seeking to
defense contractors who could guarantee him a defer-
ment. One afternoon, Hanson came in with great news:
Selective Service had ruled that all registrants with
numbers as high as his were excused. Exultant, Hanson
informed Reed that the defense firms had had their
chance, and that henceforth he would play the field,
saving himself for the highest bidder.

Its drawbacks notwithstanding, Reed told me, the
fraternity house remained a congenial home. He could
hardly hope to find such a sizable group with whom he
had more in common. No matter how narrow his
fraternity brothers' interests sometimes seemed, Reed
said, he never considered quitting their company. The
reverse, however, didn't always hold, he told me, smiling.
He discovered this in May of his final year, he said, after
President Nixon announced America's invasion of Cambodia. Reed reacted at once, convinced that a reenactment
of what he had seen in Vietnam lay in store for another
country. A few days after the President's announcement,
National Guardsmen killed four Kent State students
protesting the invasion, and Reed cast about for a way of
voicing his protest against the killings. He found it soon
enough when a minority of Tennessee students—less
than ten per cent of the school's enrollment—attended an
outdoor rally held simultaneously with demonstrations at
other colleges throughout the United States. Reed was on
the speakers' platform, the sole veteran there. The group
he addressed, Reed said, numbered about two thousand,
including large pockets of noisy, milling hecklers. The
night before the rally, while he was talking on the phone

with his parents, he mentioned what he was about to do, and his father counselled him, "Don't be too radical." In his speech, Reed, after offering his credentials as an ex-Marine, described the difficult terrain in Vietnam, the poverty of its inhabitants, and their distrust of American troops. The killings at Kent State were tantamount to "treating Americans like dinks," he said, and the entire episode was a display of raw power, of a piece with what he had seen in Vietnam. He urged the students to work for the election of representatives who would end the war forthwith. When Reed returned to his fraternity house, an enormous sign was strung across its entrance: "WE SUPPORT THE NATIONAL GUARD."

Reed wasn't through. He demonstrated again the following week, this time at Billy Graham's East Tennessee Crusade, where President Nixon was to deliver a talk. The setting was spectacular, Reed told me. For a week, he said, the East Tennessee Crusade had been in progress nightly at the state university's football stadium; over that period almost half a million Tennesseans, from Knoxville and the outlying hill country, had filled the immense amphitheatre. Many students who lived near the stadium and who were busy studying for year-end exams had sought relief from the nocturnal din by finding temporary quarters elsewhere. On the climactic evening of the Crusade, when the President was to speak, Reed and five hundred or so like-minded university students filed into the stadium. Lucy was with him, a loyal and silent partner, Reed said. Except for her, he told me, the contingent was made up of strangers, a number of whom repelled him by their long hair and stoned eyes. "It was the first I knew the campus had its freaks," he told me. The demonstrators were but a minuscule part of Graham's audience. Eighty-eight thousand people were in the stands and on the hillside around the stadium, responding enthusiastically to the revivalist's exhortations. Even the choir, brilliantly illuminated on a stage, outnumbered the demonstrators. Prior to President

Nixon's talk, Reed told me, the demonstrators engaged in a battle of hymns with the choir, singing "Jesus Loves Me" when "Onward, Christian Soldiers" issued from the choristers, or countering "Lead, Kindly Light" with "The Old Rugged Cross." While police hovered protectively, the demonstrators at several points derided Graham, their momemt of triumph coming, according to Reed, when the evangelist rebuked the demonstrators for their manners. Reed and his cohorts took particular exception to Graham's introduction of the evening's guest speaker, in which he referred to "the trying decisions" that Mr. Nixon had had to make concerning Cambodia, and then called on his followers to have faith in the President. Mr. Nixon also spoke of the need for faith, his remarks setting off waves of applause, which drowned out the demonstrators' jeers. When the President, taking note that he was speaking in a football stadium, declared that America was going to "be over that goal line before we're through," Reed and his friends shouted in unison, "Push 'em back! Shove 'em back! Wa-ay back!" Half the time, Reed remarked, he felt that he was simply engaging in a collegiate caper. He was new to political activism, he told me, and he suspected that it wasn't his thing. He had no sense of unity with his fellow-demonstrators. "I knew why I was in the stadium. I would have liked to know why each of them was there," he said.

As a result of his activism, Reed was formally censured by his fraternity brothers for "not supporting the ideals for which we strive." Denounced as a "liberal bigot" and "Wasp-hater" before the vote was taken, Reed now believed that in the first flush of their disapproval his brothers might easily have expelled him from the chapter. Two factors, however, were working for him: he was the chapter's vice-president, and just a few days earlier he had won a five-hundred-dollar prize for his scholastic record. Reed wasn't an outcast long. Two weeks intervened between the vote of censure and commencement, and in that short while, without trying, he found

himself back in everyone's good graces. This swift
change of heart was deflating to him. It made his recent
activities seem a minor aberration, which no right-think-
ing brother could take seriously: "They were letting me
know that I was one of them and that no bunch of
demonstrators could keep me off the reservation for
long."

When Reed graduated, five national firms on the
lookout for executive talent sought his services. He chose
United Metals because it offered him a chance to live in
New York. His decision, he said, yielded unexpected
results as early as his first week in the city, in the fall of
1970. Hunting for an apartment, he inspected one
together with a competitor—a slight twenty-year-old boy
on crutches who was wearing a large button with the
words "VIETNAM VETERANS AGAINST THE WAR." "My
eyes popped," Reed told me. "Down in Knoxville, people
didn't go around with buttons like that." The apartment
proved too expensive for each of the young men, and they
left together. As soon as they were outside, Reed pointed
to the stranger's button and said, "I'm a Vietnam veteran
and I'm against the war." The stranger, Pierre Minot,
explained that his button bore the name of an organization to which he belonged. He urged Reed to join the
V.V.A.W., which, he said, favored an immediate end to
the war and the recall of all American troops, an
investigation of "American war crimes," and legislation
providing for job training and placement of returning
veterans. In Minot's opinion, such influence as the
organization exerted derived from the fact that its
members clearly spoke about the war with a certain
authority. "It would be hard for anyone to call us draft
dodgers," he said, smiling. On the street that day, the two
became friends. Like Reed, Minot had been in the
Marines. North Vietnamese shrapnel had shattered his
left leg, severing many nerves. When he wasn't working
for the V.V.A.W., he was a patient in a Veterans

Administration hospital in downtown Manhattan, where
neurologists hoped to restore a degree of sensation in his
damaged leg.

In the months since they had known each other, Reed
told me one day as we were talking in his apartment, he
had frequently visited Minot in the hospital—which, he
added, Minot had reentered a couple of days before.
Consulting his watch, Reed suggested we go see him.
"It's visiting hours," he said. He left a note for his absent
roommate, and we were on our way. In a downtown bus,
Reed told me that after his first encounter with Minot he
had gone down to the V.V.A.W. headquarters, then on
lower Fifth Avenue, and met a number of the members,
many of whom had differing political outlooks. Some of
them, like his fellow-demonstrators in the Tennessee
stadium, Reed said, repelled him by their youth-culture
trappings. Nevertheless, he told me, he eagerly and
happily joined the organization, because it enabled him
to meet Vietnam veterans who, like himself, had been
carrying corroding memories. At long last, he said, he was
able to share his own with those of other men who had
fought in Indo-China. Many of them, it seemed to him,
had endured far more harrowing experiences than he had.
It brought him a freeing excitement, he said, to hear
younger veterans—those who had come after him—unin-
hibitedly condemn the patriotic performances they had
given. Perhaps mistakenly, Reed saw in this proof that
men in his outfit had felt the same as he had when they
had all been in Vietnam. "We just didn't talk. When we
were there, the government still seemed a pillar," he said.

As the bus approached midtown, Reed told me that the
V.V.A.W. had emerged for him as a second fraternity.
Many of the friends he had in New York came from its
ranks, he said, but, he added, they weren't his only
friends. He also had some at United Metals, and, of
course, his older friends in Knoxville and back home in
Cedarville. "I've never mixed the two sets," he said. He
was in a different world with each, he went on, by which

he didn't mean to imply that the people at United Metals
with small flags on their desks never deplored the war.
They did, he said, but within bounds—without challenging the prerogatives of the government or "the system," as
some V.V.A.W. members did. At United Metals, he said,
there was chafing, occasionally, over the great outlay of
men and money the United States had made in
Indo-China without much to show for it. In this, Reed
suggested, he didn't think his office colleagues were so
different from Americans generally, including most New
Yorkers. He himself, he said, took no stock in polls
indicating widespread discontent with the war; in the
unlikely event that South Vietnamese troops were to score
a few victories in the field, he believed it might well turn
the polls around. The opposition of the veterans he knew,
though, was of an entirely different quality. They felt
angered and violated by what they had been called upon
to do in Indo-China. It came out clearly, Reed thought, at
so-called rap sessions that took place Saturday afternoons
at the V.V.A.W. offices; at the sessions in which Reed
participated, the veterans talked of their recent past.
Glancing out the bus window, Reed said that he
considered the veterans' opposition to the war far more
deep-seated than that of outsiders. He was troubled,
though, he said, by the veterans' abiding anger. It
provided an important bond, he realized, but it was
without plan. At United Metals, an entirely different
atmosphere prevailed, he said. Anger was no staple there,
and unquestionably, he said, the company's headquarters
in the Chrysler Building were charged with purpose—its
objectives, of course, the making of metal products and of
profits. Perhaps, Reed said, the mammoth firm, with its
orderliness and efficiency, reminded him at times of the
reliability he had imputed to the government in his
pre-Vietnam days.

In the hospital lobby, guards asked Reed and me to
state our business; they were on the alert for pushers
peddling drugs to the patients. On Minot's floor, walking

along the corridor toward his ward, we encountered a fair
number of men in wheelchairs, among them some young
amputees. The ages of the men we saw covered a wide
range—from the First World War to the Vietnam war. We
passed a glass-enclosed lounge where a dozen veterans
were viewing a Western on a color television set; one of
the group was a black—he seemed to be a teen-ager
—whose head was swathed in a turban of white
bandages. As we entered Minot's ward, Reed waved to
another young black man; the patient was on methadone,
I later learned from Reed, who had met him on past visits
to Minot. The ward had about thirty beds, most of them
empty; their occupants might have been among the
patients we had seen in the corridor and lounge. Except
for a family gathered near the bed of a middle-aged
veteran, Reed and I were the only visitors. When we
reached Minot's bed, we found him meticulously sewing
the rigging of a model schooner, which rested on a mobile
table across his bed. He had on a thimble and was
cross-eyed with concentration. Reed had to clear his
throat to attract his attention.

"Hey, man!" Minot exclaimed. He and Reed exchanged
smiles before I was introduced. "Welcome to the jungle,"
Minot greeted me, his hand indicating the ward. A thin,
sallow boy, he spoke shyly, with a slight French accent;
Reed had told me his parents came from Martinique.
Alongside Minot's bed were his crutches and a wheelchair, into which Reed dropped. I fetched myself an
ordinary chair. The patient in the bed opposite Minot's, a
man in his fifties, was muttering loudly to himself. He
had a small television set of his own; it was on, but the
man lay with his back to it. "He'll calm down," Minot
said. In a little while, the man did. Minot told us that his
neighbor had been a master sergeant on Guadalcanal in
the Second World War. Minot grinned. "He calls his war
the Big Deuce," he said to Reed. "He says ours is just a
police action." The summer before, Minot went on, he
and other Vietnam veterans sunning themselves in

wheelchairs on the hospital grounds had been jeered at by several passing pedestrians, whose age Minot judged to have been about thirty-five. "They called us 'suckers' and 'jerks,'" he said. "They were right, but it was a hell of a thing to listen to." Minot was a hundred-per-cent-disability case. He had been in Vietnam three months before becoming a casualty, and since then he had spent more than a year in hospitals, Minot told me. He had no idea what the neurologists would say this time about his leg. Proudly, he informed me of the precise medical term for his condition. He had been laid up so much, he said, that he had finally become interested in medicine. Depending on his health, he was planning to become a paramedical worker, but first, he said, he wanted to devote all his energies to ending the war. He and Reed discussed V.V.A.W. projects—fund raising, demonstrations, parades.

When their shoptalk was over, Reed remarked that he wouldn't be in again for a few weeks. "I'm getting married," he said.

The younger man laughed and said, "Now that's what I call straight. I'll bet you're even having a honeymoon."

Reed nodded, and replied, "In the Caribbean. And I don't like warm weather."

Minot laughed again. Reed emptied his pockets of a half-dozen packs of cigarettes he had brought Minot. The Guadalcanal sergeant had fallen asleep; the image on his television screen had gone haywire. Reed and I started to say goodbye, and Minot announced that he wanted to see us off at the elevator. He needed his wheelchair, he told Reed, who slowly—almost, it seemed, reluctantly—rose from it. In the next instant, Minot swung with incongruous grace into the wheelchair.

The following Saturday, Reed arranged for me to sit in on a rap session in one of three rooms that made up the V.V.A.W.'s modest headquarters on lower Fifth Avenue. Eight other veterans were there, and so were two psychiatrists, all of us jammed into a cubicle that was part storage room for bundles of V.V.A.W. literature, a movie projector, and a duplicating machine. We were deployed around a battered wooden table. Four veterans lounged uncomfortably on top of the bundles or on the sill of a window that faced the blank, begrimed wall of another building. At the time of my visit, sessions of this sort had been going on for four months, and were being regularly attended by psychiatrists who were studying the veterans' reactions to the war. The two psychiatrists on hand were both university professors. One of them hardly spoke. The other, a man with an air of sly profundity, occasionally interjected comments like "I sense hostility here, but I do not hear it expressed." Nearly all of the veterans had seen combat; several of them had been wounded. Except for one newcomer, they knew each other from previous sessions and talked freely, moving easily from topic to topic. Reed, at twenty-six, was probably the old man among them. He certainly seemed almost fatherly toward an ex-Marine, Chris Anderson, a boyish-looking Texan, who was given to making extravagant assertions. When the others jumped on Anderson, Reed would protect him, apparently persuaded that Anderson might still be in a state of youthful upheaval. I was interested, too, to see Reed's blue eyes light up when at one point in the proceedings a Navy man, whose gunboat had patrolled the Mekong River, spoke of having tried to know the Vietnamese as individuals. "I didn't want to think of them as B-girls and hookers," the Navy man said. "I would try to make friends with children. If they liked me, I might get to meet their mothers and fathers."

There was no ostensible form to the session, its content being a mixture of random military recollections and responses to civilian life. In tone, though, it may have had a certain cohesion, for, throughout, the men reflected a bewilderment that they could have served their country without serving a discernible cause. Several veterans compared their service to the unreality of movies. One said, "When we were attacking near Dak To, guys were falling to my left and right, and I remember telling myself, 'Just keep going, like John Wayne.'" Parents were often mentioned at the session, usually for their inability to grasp the depth of their sons' anger about the war. "When my father heard me talk about the war, he was convinced I'd flipped my lid," one veteran testified. The consensus in the room was that such parents had imagined that their children would return firm believers in the government for which they had just fought. One veteran in the group said that he had considered himself a perfectly solid citizen on his return, but that he had been given a hard time by a kid brother who had turned anti-war activist. The veteran, a former Army medical corpsman, said, "We had terrible arguments. I felt betrayed." The brothers became reconciled only after the ex-corpsman began to have second thoughts about his military service. He said, "I started remembering things I'd done to P.O.W.s, like pulling their teeth without Novocain for no damn reason."

There were many references to "the system." Without exception, it was personal situations that appeared to inspire use of the sweeping term. For instance, Anderson invoked it because his homecoming had been a disappointment. He related that two years earlier he had arrived home unexpectedly from the war to find his parents giving a party; they had moved to a different city in Texas while he was gone, and now, introducing him around to their new friends, they boasted of his heroic exploits. Initially, Anderson said, the praise had embarrassed him, but he soon saw that he had no cause for embarrassment. "Nobody there seemed to care," he told his fellow-veterans. "All they wanted to know from me was who would take the Super Bowl game. They were deep into bridge, bowling leagues—all that Pablum. I went out to the yard and stayed there." A few days later, leaving his uniform behind, Anderson had taken off in a used M.G. that he had bought with some of his Marine pay. After a run of six hundred miles, the car's engine burned out in the business section of a small town in the Texas panhandle. A deputy sheriff, happening by, eyed Anderson's hair, which hadn't been cut since he had left Khe Sanh, two months previously. The deputy frisked him and found a souvenir of Vietnam—the last quarter ounce of some marijuana he had brought back. After being defended by a court-appointed lawyer, Anderson spent forty-seven days in jail, where, he said, he frequently thought about the time he had done at Khe Sanh during the siege. The unconcern of the Americans he had seen since he had returned was also on his mind. He said, "If they can't care about the lousy, senseless things we had to do, then I'm a Vietcong in my own country. It's either them or me, and if the system doesn't change, and soon, I'm going to disappear. I'll go underground. I'll find other Vietcong there."

There was an immediate outcry in the room. The veterans knew that Anderson was talking violence, and they wanted no part of it. Speaking quietly, a former Army Intelligence agent named Miller said to Anderson, "You must have a good reason for being at this rap session, and not making bombs." An earnest, intellectual-looking young man with curly black hair, Miller was a Harvard graduate who had majored in government. He waited patiently for a response from Anderson, but there wasn't any.

Solicitously, Reed intervened. "Chris is here for the same reason the rest of us are," he said. "He's upset over what we did in Vietnam, and he wants his country to stop bullying the hell out of people."

Miller paid no attention. Almost gently, he asked Anderson, "What kind of life would you like?"

This time, Anderson answered. "I could do with a place in Texas near a creek," he said. "I'd like to raise horses and some cattle."

Before the session was over, Reed himself came under

attack. This occurred when he was challenged to
reconcile his anti-war views with working for United
Metals, a firm that was filling war contracts. The question
made Reed ill at ease, and his answer, given defensively,
left most of his listeners dissatisfied. He said, "I'd rather
my company didn't have those contracts, but sometimes
you have to neutralize your integrity. I want a career,
which maybe some of you guys don't, and I can't see
myself telling my boss, 'Let's forget our competitors.
Let's not make missiles, just pots and pans.' Besides, I
don't sign contracts. I'm low man at my firm. I find
parking space for senior execs."

The others in the room—at least those who had jobs
—didn't have Reed's problem. Anderson worked on a
horse farm near the tip of Long Island. A veteran whose
face was barely visible for his hair was a bookkeeper at a
large discount establishment. An ex-Navy man was
awaiting appointment by the Federal Aviation Administration as a sky marshal—a job that he characterized as "a
symptom of our paranoid society." A Puerto Rican who
identified himself only as Juan had a job delivering milk
at night; it was quiet work, he said, for which he was
thankful. Juan was at his first rap session, and he was glad
to be there. "I've been talking about Vietnam for three
years, mostly to deaf people," he said. He had been a
paratrooper, and everyone in his original company had
been killed or wounded. One casualty in particular stood
out in his mind, and, unburdening himself, he told the
group about a buddy called Tommy, who had saved his
life while they were on a night patrol. The following
week, when Juan was asleep in a foxhole, a rat had
nibbled at one of his ears, and he had been sent to a rear
area for a plague shot. While he was gone, Tommy had
been killed by Vietcong. Back with his unit, Juan had
fought wildly—"to make it up to Tommy," he said. He
had finally been hit by a sniper. "I believe my mind is all
fouled up," he concluded.

Immediately, one of the psychiatrists informed Juan

that "survival guilt" was a common consequence of all wars, particularly ones "whose purpose is poorly understood."

Speaking less abstractly, others in the group assured Juan that they had had similar experiences. One veteran told Juan that he owed his life to a buddy who had been killed alongside him and whose corpse had shielded him from a stream of enemy bullets. A former infantry sergeant said he lived with the memory of dispatching four G.I.s on a mission of doubtful value and then learning that the patrol had been wiped out. Shocked by the news, the sergeant had sought the guidance of the chaplain. "I found him blessing artillery pieces," the sergeant said.

Groaning, another veteran exclaimed, "Chaplains—oh, my God!" Everyone seemed to have a story about chaplains. "Ours used to give us pep talks before we went on sweeps," Juan said, his spirits rising. One of the ex-Navy men told of a graveside service he had attended; the presiding chaplain had called on the assembled mourners to avenge the departed with an improved kill ratio. Making the same point his colleague had, the second psychiatrist suggested that it might have been difficult for chaplains to lend spiritual counsel when the members of their flocks were fighting without comprehension.

The men talked of how they had felt on going off to war. They spoke almost ritualistically, as though in salute to the magnitude of events they would remember the rest of their lives. The sky-marshal candidate said he had been gung ho on leaving for Indo-China. "I believed that if I survived I would come back an enlarged person," he told the group. "But I didn't expect to come back. In the bus on the way to the airport, I looked out the window and told myself, 'That may be the last red Mustang I'll ever see.'"

Another veteran said he had counted on a heart murmur to spare him Army service. "When they took me, I nearly had a heart attack," he said. Miller was the one who talked longest about his military service. He was the only one of the veterans, it developed, who had been opposed to the war before putting on a uniform. At Harvard, he said, he had read every book on Vietnam he could find, analyzed with classmates the American presence there, and concluded that the war was a moral and political disaster. In the end, though, he told the group, he had been swayed by the fact that his parents had come to America as refugees from Nazi Germany. They had brought him up to be grateful for a government that didn't mount pogroms. Miller spoke fluent French, and upon being drafted was quickly shipped to Vietnam for intelligence assignments that would exploit this asset. That was in 1969—a year before our invasion of Cambodia. His activities, he said, were concerned with subverting that then supposedly neutral state. "We were running intelligence agents into Cambodia," Miller said. "They were mostly old French officers, left over from colonial days." Everyone in on the operation, including Miller, was ordered to dream up a cover name. Miller laughed dryly. "I called myself Levy. It was the bravest thing I did," he said. In Indo-China, Miller continued, he discovered daily that he had got his wars mixed up; he wasn't in the one that he had thought he owed his country. He was incensed with himself for having failed to resist the draft. To mitigate the feeling, he said, he had never carried a gun; that meant he couldn't kill anyone. Sharply, he told the group, "We've been had, and our so-called leaders have to know it from us. They have to know they can't ever get away with the same thing again. If the government is still worth a damn, it's the last favor we can do it."

The following Saturday afternoon, I was at Reed's apartment. He was avoiding the weekly rap session. He doubted whether he would attend any more. The sessions rattled him, he said, leaving him each time with the

impression that he had only two choices: to be a "social
dropout" or to take "the pig route," as scornful
fellow-veterans labelled his career at United Metals. He
said he could probably earn their plaudits—for whatever
they were worth—by becoming, say, an itinerant auto
mechanic. Reed looked at Lucy's photograph on the small
bookcase. He was leaving for Tennessee in two days to
marry her; fraternity brothers would be at the wedding in
force. The apartment awaited her ministrations. Emerson
Hayes had moved out, taking his furniture, and the place
was bare. All it had was a canvas cot, on which Reed and I
were sitting; a phone, beside him on the floor; the
initiation paddles on the walls; and the bookcase, whose
contents were concerned exclusively with Vietnam.
Planning was absurd, he said, but for the present he and
Lucy were letting themselves imitate the ways of their
parents, without conviction. He and Lucy couldn't live
on slogans. He would persevere at United Metals,
regardless of what some V.V.A.W. members thought.
Today wasn't the first time he had stayed away from a rap
session, he said. He had moments, in fact, when he
wondered why he couldn't be like most veterans and not
bother with any organization. But, whatever the
V.V.A.W.'s faults, he told me, being in it sustained in him
a sense that he had not yet numbed himself to what he
had seen in Vietnam. He didn't want that to happen. "It
would be like walking away from a bad accident," he
said. Nor did he want the rewards of business success, if
he achieved them, to erode his memories. He wished he
had the gumption to follow his instincts. "I'd be a
married priest," he said.

Whenever the war might end, Reed believed that its
impact on him would continue long afterward. He had no
idea how its details would eventually unfold for him, but,
broadly, he knew that his attitude toward the government
had undergone a profound change since his arrival in
Danang in 1965. Reed now spoke as rancorously as Miller
had at the previous week's rap session. "Our country is

just not as great and wonderful as I thought it was," he said. "The integrity of our leaders in Washington hasn't been what I was brought up to expect. They tricked an entire population into a war. I'm glad we're not winning in Vietnam. It would make us more trigger-happy than we are. We'd go powering into the Middle East, or you name it, and we're not all that unbeatable." He hated mistrusting the government, he said. It deprived him of a foundation stone. It imposed on him an interest in politics that he didn't want. When he had thought about it, Reed told me, he had envisioned a life of private pursuits, with public cares, so to speak, entrusted to the good offices of the government. That was all changed now. He had no recourse but to turn political, at least by his standards, for the government, he said, had revealed that it could overreach itself by asking for lives when there was no need for them. But the war hadn't entirely transformed him. It hadn't left him a pacifist, he said, as Lucy sometimes thought it had. He would fight again if he believed America was truly in danger, and he was capable of saying this, he told me, only because he retained a hope that the country might regain its better side as a result of the war. "I know it's nothing to bet on," he said, "but neither is anything else I can think of."

4

THE SUPREME OPTION

During those wartime days when American fortunes in Asia were still in the balance, when the President warned the North Vietnamese that they were courting "grave risks" and threatened, as he did in December, 1970, to "destroy" military sites and supporting areas in North Vietnam, it crossed my mind—and no doubt the minds of other Americans—that eventually the United States might choose to drop an atom bomb on Indo-China. It was a deeply disquieting speculation, but one, alas, that was founded in the past behavior of nations. When was it in pre-nuclear times that a country locked in combat with another failed to let fly with its most powerful weapon? What was going on in Vietnam in 1970 that the United States should refrain from totally demolishing its enemy? Given America's use of napalm, aerial explosives, and howitzers in that distant land, would it have made any essential difference if the United States resorted to nuclear bombs? Like everyone else, I was aware that their destructive force far exceeded that of ordinary explosives, but what was one to make of this? That nuclear bombs had made the world safe for so-called conventional warfare? Prompted by such questions, I tried to find out why it was that the United States hadn't unloosed what was considered its knockout punch.

In Washington, I talked with numerous officials of the Nixon Administration as well as of the preceding one, including former Secretary of State Dean Rusk. My interviews took me to the Pentagon, to the State Department, and to Capitol Hill, where one of the legislators I saw at some length was Representative Chet Holifield, the chairman of the Joint Congressional Committee on Atomic Energy. In academic communities far from Washington, I talked with political and physical scientists—individuals without governmental ties who had devoted long study to the riddles of arms control. In addition, I talked with consultants of the Rand Corporation, a think tank in Santa Monica, California, whose thinkers sought answers to policy questions confronting the Air Force and other federal agencies. Though these men and women were often in disagreement with one another, they gave the impression of holding membership in a closed club, their principal qualification being an assiduous, and admirable, willingness to "think about the unthinkable"; it was this , more than anything else, that marked them as experts. A few demurred at discussing the efficacy of dropping the bomb. "People might get worried," one told me, evidently persuaded that the country's prevailing mood was a carefree one. In the main, though, the experts proved cooperative, apprising me of many complexities that would have necessarily attended the release of a "nuke," in the trade term. These complexities were often dilemma-ridden—so much so that in the course of my interviewing I heard more than one expert wonder aloud whether owning these weapons was not more risk than advantage. Touching on this, a biochemistry professor told me, "Use a nuke and you go from an analytical situation to a mythological one, from tested military doctrine to an uncharted realm where it's only dreams that count."

According to a "back-of-the-envelope estimate" given me by a former Defense Department official, four hundred one-megaton bombs would destroy every structure in North Vietnam and every one of the twenty-one million people there. None of his fellow-experts disputed the estimate, although most of them seemed to have their own pet formulas for achieving the same result. No one doubted that nukes could quickly and expeditiously lay North Vietnam open to invasion. Less sweepingly, some confined themselves to explaining how nuclear weapons could be used to close off mountain roads that were vital to the southward movement of enemy troops and equipment. Hanoi's war effort would be seriously hampered, I was informed, if the Mu Gia Pass, which winds through Laos at the north end of the Ho Chi Minh Trail, were sealed. An Air Force man told me, "We've dumped tons of conventional stuff there, but it hasn't given us the massive rockslides we need." It was also suggested to me that nuclear weapons could enable the United States to place a radioactive curtain across the Demilitarized Zone, making it impenetrable to the North Vietnamese ground troops. In the Red River Delta, not far from the Chinese border, I learned, there was an attractive target consisting of a network of dikes covering several hundred square miles, the destruction of which could cause a catastrophic flooding of agricultural lands. Haiphong, North Vietnam's main harbor for receiving foreign supplies, could be demolished beyond repair. The same fate could overtake Hanoi, with its one million two hundred thousand inhabitants—not that anyone I interviewed saw much military point in this. Conventional weapons could also do great damage to the capital, I was told, but they would not pack the "shock value" of nukes. "There's nothing like them for demoralizing an enemy," a mild-mannered physicist at M.I.T. said.

No one advocated, in so many words, that the United States employ an atomic bomb. Even those few individuals who, in 1970, still thought in terms of victory were inclined to grant that a nuclear bomb might start a chain of ungovernable consequences. Predicting one such possibility, a Harvard professor of international affairs told me, "Even if it were only an unpopulated section of the Mu Gia Pass that we hit, there would be reactions —both violent and nonviolent—here in the United States the like of which we've never known. The demonstrators would take up acres." Abroad, it was foreseen, not only would a similar outcry arise but the leaders of foreign governments would be quick to heed it sympathetically. Most of the experts I saw believed that Britain, for one, would withdraw forthwith from NATO, the key to America's system for defending Western Europe from Russian invasion. "The only allies we'd have left would be military dictatorships like Spain and Greece," a retired ambassador told me.

In Asia, it was stated, the United States would suddenly appear in a different light. "In the Orient, they think of us as having the stamina to see things through, with a little left over in reserve," a State Department analyst told me. American alliances there would be devalued. For the Japanese, painful historical memories would be aroused. Nor would the nationals of other Asian countries fail to realize that once again the United States had used a nuclear weapon against a yellow people. Thailand and Indonesia would be eager to get out from under Washington's wing, which would seem anything but protective; every Asian nation that had been friendly would dread experiencing Indo-China's fate. "And I certainly wouldn't want to be in Saigon," the State Department man remarked. He went on to point out that it would be a simple matter for the other side to retaliate by smuggling a bomb into the South Vietnamese capital. A cyclist could do it, or a boatman in an innocuous-looking sampan. Even a slow, outmoded plane could suffice

as a delivery vehicle, my informant said, for American
forces were so accustomed to monopolizing the Vietnamese skies that they would probably mistake the aircraft for one of their own.

But nuclear reprisal was far too momentous a development to happen covertly. If it came, the experts said, it
would signal Russian intervention on Hanoi's behalf, and
America's rival superpower, like, America itself, wasn't
given to fooling around with bicycles and sampans but
with ICBMs and submarines, multiple warheads and
early-warning systems. As for China, it was discounted
for the moment as a full-fledged nuclear force, although
no one doubted that it would soon be one. Reprisal, or the
imminent prospect of it, I was told, would surely set off a
wave of bomb-building in countries that had not yet gone
nuclear. Fearful of becoming nuclear battlefields, these
countries would see acquiring bombs of their own as
their only means of self-protection. A weapons researcher
at the Livermore Laboratory, in California, who discussed this with me said that in 1960 it had been expected
that by 1970 there would be fifteen nations with nukes,
and that this hadn't come about because so far the
superpowers had deterred each other from using the
weapons. He added, "As long as that holds, other
countries figure they may as well save themselves the
expense of going nuclear."

Reprisal could easily lead to an exchange of nuclear
strikes between the United States and the Soviet Union,
but the resulting casualties would be so appalling that,
according to government officials, the United States, for
its part, might not necessarily hit back even if a limited
attack on the American mainland cost the United States as
many as ten million dead. The government would first
want to investigate the nature of the impact, which might
have been accidental, and then explore the possibility of
calling a halt to nuclear shooting. But if an all-out
exchange—"wargasm," in the jargon—were to take place,
it would end, in Mr. Rusk's words, "with a handful of

miserable survivors contemplating the folly of man." On
the subject of casualties, Ambassador Cyrus R. Vance, a
former Deputy Secretary of Defense, said, "When you
stop to think of their numbers, you're simply in another
world." The estimates I heard most frequently were that
blast and radiation would account for a total of two
hundred million deaths in both the United States and
Russia, and fire and fallout might kill almost everyone
else in the two countries. Government officials told me
that both the White House and the Kremlin regarded
casualties of this magnitude as "unacceptable." In the
mind of one expert, it wasn't at all certain that retaliation
would necessarily occur even if orders for it were given.
The expert was Paul C. Warnke, a former Assistant
Secretary of Defense, who said, "If one superpower were
to hit another with everything it had, I can well imagine
submarine commanders lying at the bottom of the sea and
wondering whether to carry out their pre-planned orders
to strike back. With their country and their families gone,
suicide might seem attractive."

Practically everybody I talked with doubted that nukes
would be used in Indo-China. For one thing, the terrain
was too densely covered with jungle to permit the spread
of the immense fires that accompany atomic bombings.
Another mitigating factor was the modesty of Hanoi's war
effort, which, it was explained, gave the enemy great
mobility and resilience. Discussing this, a well-known
"defense intellectual" who had served under Secretary
McNamara told me that if a nuke destroyed Hanoi the
North Vietnamese would carry on from their back
country. "They don't need a capital," he said. "Their
leaders have right along wanted the war on the
ground—the ground that's familiar to their people.
Bigness isn't their style. The smaller the scale of
operations, the better it suits their temperament."
Conversely, it was said, America's flair for bigness made
it extremely vulnerable in Vietnam; if Hanoi were able to

mount a sizable attack—even one consisting of conventional weapons—the enormous bases that the United States had constructed would present fat, concentrated targets. Another authority who felt that an atomic bomb wouldn't be very useful in Indo-China was an important Pentagon scientist, a man widely known in Washington as Dr. Strangelove. Addressing himself solely to the problem of killing enemy troops, he emphasized their talent for concealment and dispersal. A nuclear weapon, he insisted, would not work well against invisible troops numbering only a few hundred per square mile. Small targets called for small ordnance, he went on, and it did not have to be nuclear. Speaking vigorously, he said, "Bomblets! Clusters of those little bombs—that's what works in Vietnam. In that place, I'll take a thousand one-pound hunks of exploding steel any day over a single thousand-pounder. One of those hunks is sure to search out the target you're after. There's no wasteful overkill to bomblets—just a nice, uniform distribution of energy."

In these discussions, the initial responses to my question about using nuclear bombs in Indo-China were invariably of a pragmatic sort. No one raised the question of moral objections. When I myself did, however, responses were quickly forthcoming. A well-known statesman commented, "In diplomacy, one prefers to say 'political,' which I believe absorbs your word 'moral.'" A senior fellow at the Brookings Institution, in Washington, thought of morality as method, describing it as "flat rules of generalization based on practical reasons." Occasionally, the responses had a defensive note, as in the case of a Rand physicist who denounced a Harvard professor for having refused to do any further work as a consultant for the National Security Council in protest over the American invasion of Cambodia. The Rand man said, "Imagine his acting holier than thou! Why, he's written the most cold-blooded battle scenarios I've ever read!" General Maxwell D. Taylor's reaction was to defend his profession from any and all insinuations. "I have never heard a military man propose the use of a nuclear weapon," he told me. The late Robert F. Kennedy bore different witness. Describing a White House conference in "Thirteen Days," his account of the Cuban missile crisis, in 1962, he wrote, "One member of the Joint Chiefs of Staff, for example, argued that we could use nuclear weapons, on the basis that our adversaries would use theirs against us in an attack. I thought, as I listened, of the many times that I had heard the military take positions which, if wrong, had the advantage that no one would be around at the end to know."

More often than not, I found that my mention of moral aspects drew silence, some people eying me warily or waiting indulgently for me to get on with the day's business. There were those, however, in whom my query seemed to rekindle old crusading fires, and the burden of their sentiments was that whatever it was that had thus far inhibited the nuclear powers from dropping an atomic bomb constituted the firebreak that was keeping the world in one piece. If an atomic bomb were to fall in Vietnam, they said, it would destroy not only its target but the hope that Hiroshima had bequeathed a life-preserving taboo. Illusory or not, it was said, once its sanctity was violated, nuclear weapons would acquire the status of standard, or conventional, instruments of warmaking. "They must be regarded as weapons of last resort, on which there lies a curse," Mr. Rusk, a principal architect of the Vietnam war, told me. "As Secretary of State, I was determined that while I was in office no nuclear weapon would be fired in anger. It is a quarter of a century since that has occurred. The country that ends that interval will carry the mark of Cain on its brow for the rest of its history."

Inevitably, perhaps, the attitude of young people was brought into the conversations. Young people, it was said, had a tendency to think in terms of moral absolutes, and this might do more harm than good in respect to nuclear weapons. One State Department official discussed the thinking of his undergraduate son: "All or none, good or evil, that's the way he and his friends argue. They lump nukes with napalm. It's idealistic, sure—until a nuke hits Vietnam, or anywhere else." A middle-aged senator told me that young people think of the Second World War "as though it were bygone history, like the Wars of the Roses," and said he feared that this outlook might result in a relaxation of America's present controls over the use of nuclear weapons. After pointing out that almost half the American population had yet to be born at the time of Japan's surrender, he went on, "The average age of us legislators is fifty-four, so most of us can remember the shock we knew when Hiroshima was wiped out. But there's no way we can pass that memory on to the young people who are going to be sitting where we now are."

A few semesters ago, Professor I. I. Rabi, a Nobel laureate in physics, gave a special course at Columbia for gifted students in science and other fields who had evinced interest in the social and philosophical implications of twentieth-century physics, and he told me that he had found it a dispiriting experience. The students didn't recognize the so-called "ultimate weapon" as a unique menace to the species. "They kept spouting that society was corrupt," Dr. Rabi told me. Conceivably, he suggested, the students may have imagined that there was no chance of the bomb's ever being used again. "Many older people think that, too. It's a mistake," he continued. "It leaves out human nature. We're always tempted to hope that problems will go away, and here we are, still faced with those Russian and Asian problems, after spending so much treasure on weaponry. Are we Americans all that exceptional? Aren't we just as capable as anyone else of finally getting fed up?"

Though the consensus was definitely that the United States would refrain from using atomic bombs in Indo-China, the experts often hedged on their assertions, making the point that the country was in an "unusual" war and that there was no telling how it would end. In

1970, one imponderable that appeared to be very much on the minds of several of them had to do with the American pullout from Vietnam that was then under way. Paradoxically, perhaps, they saw the pullout not as a harbinger of peace but as a dangerous gamble that might radically intensify the fighting. These people expressed concern over the fact that the pullout had been initiated at a moment when the war could scarcely be described as running in America's favor. It was no time for the United States to weaken itself, they maintained, and if it continued to do so while being fought to a standstill it might be asking for an American Dunkirk. Elaborating on this, a State Department consultant said to me, "What will be done when we get down to between a hundred thousand and zero men in Vietnam? No scenario for that has yet been worked through, but do it yourself. Here's the situation: The enemy is closing in on our troops, who are outnumbered and trapped. Think of the domestic pressures that would be exerted on the President. Think of the Joint Chiefs of Staff telling the country they need a free hand to save our boys. Think of the bind the President would be in. Whoever he is, he might not find it unthinkable to drop a nuke."

I was reminded that the spectre of a glorious nuclear retreat had already loomed before in Vietnam. In 1954, when the French were besieged at Dien Bien Phu, Admiral Arthur W. Radford, Chairman of the Joint Chiefs of Staff, suggested that the United States could rescue them with nuclear wapons. Fourteen years later—in the winter of 1968—high-ranking officers were reported to have applied similar pressure on President Johnson when five thousand American Marines appeared to be hopelessly surrounded at Khe Sanh. As the Marines' plight grew worse, press dispatches made it increasingly clear that military commanders in Vietnam wanted permission to use nuclear weapons. In America, senators confirmed the reports. The British Prime Minister, Harold Wilson, voiced alarm while he was on an official visit in the United States. Many private initiatives were undertaken, among them one by three eminent scientists—Professor Rabi, Professor George B. Kistiakowsky, of Harvard, and Dr. James R. Killian, chairman of the corporation of M.I.T. Both Kistiakowsky and Killian had served as chief science adviser to President Eisenhower. Taking advantage of this relationship, the three scientists sent the following telegram to General Eisenhower, then on a winter holiday in Palm Springs, California:

PRIVATE AND CONFIDENTIAL.

THE IMPLICATIONS OF CURRENT PUBLIC STATEMENTS BY SOME GOVERNMENT SPOKESMEN COULD BE THAT USE OF NUCLEAR WEAPONS IN VIETNAM SPECIFICALLY AROUND KHE SANH IS TO BE CONSIDERED IF OUR MILITARY SITUATION WORSENS. WE ARE DEEPLY CONCERNED ABOUT GRAVE AND IMMEDIATE DANGER THAT THE ENEMY WOULD RECIPROCATE AGAINST OUR FLEET AND VULNERABLE SHORE FACILITIES AND THAT THIS EXCHANGE DISADVANTAGEOUS TO US COULD LEAD TO GENERAL NUCLEAR WAR. IN ADDITION OUR USE OF SUCH WEAPONS WILL DO IRREPARABLE DAMAGE TO OUR INTERNATIONAL POSITION INCLUDING PROGRESS OF THE NON-PROLIFERATION TREATY AND TO DOMESTIC TRANQUILLITY. WE RESPECTFULLY RECOMMEND THAT YOU URGE ON ADMINISTRATION SUCH MILITARY POLICIES IN VIETNAM AS TO MAKE THE USE OF NUCLEAR WEAPONS ASSUREDLY UNNECESSARY.

IF YOU WISH ANY ONE OF US WOULD HAPPILY COME TO PRESENT DETAILED CONSIDERATIONS.

WARM PERSONAL REGARDS.

Fortuitously, just after the telegram reached Palm Springs, President Johnson arrived to visit General Eisenhower, who showed him the message. Three days later, Secretary McNamara phoned each of the scientists to dispel his fears about Khe Sanh. Afterward, thanking

General Eisenhower for his intervention, Professor Kistiakowsky wrote, "Of course [Secretary McNamara] was in no position to say anything about the future."

In the final analysis, it is the President alone who, as Commander-in-Chief, has the power to decide whether an American nuclear bomb shall be dropped. It is a fearsome privacy. Wherever the President travels, he is shadowed by "the man with the football," an individual whose single function is to carry a bag holding a variety of codes that pertain to the release—or recall—of one or more bombs. On any given day, a President knows, a Soviet warhead may land here fifteen minutes after its launching, and in those minutes he will have to make up his mind about our response, if any, with or without consulting his Russian counterpart on the hot line. In that pressured interval, the comprehensive briefings that all Presidents are periodically given by military and scientific instructors must stand him in good stead. It is then that he must choose from the repertory of "contingency plans" he has been taught— plans that are in large part the product of so-called war games, in which random teams of government officials, armed with computers, have done battle in Pentagon conference rooms.

A President is under no obligation to seek congressional approval of a decision to use atomic weapons; nor, several congressmen told me, is he likely to, since it would only invite debate and perhaps keep the President from following his own best judgment. "No President cares to give up options," one New York legislator assured me. Thus, if a President sees fit to do so, he may order the launching of a nuclear missile. A high-ranking officer told me that the chances are slim that his companions at the time would try to talk him out of it. "The President would want sympathetic souls around, fellows who saw things the way he did," he said. For all practical purposes, then, a President is answerable solely to his own tenets of responsibility in using the bomb, and these, needless to say, vary from President to President. John F. Kennedy, for example, was remembered by one man I talked to as having possessed an "internalized" determination never to release a bomb—a resolve that was severely tested during the Cuban missile crisis. Mr. Risk told me, "John Kennedy never brooded over the possibility of assassination, but he did brood over the thought that certain situations might cause him to press the button." In the opinion of Professor Thomas C. Schelling, of the Harvard Center for International Affairs, a President who is genuinely resistant to the idea of using nuclear weapons will treat the possibility with "a ritualistic abhorrence" and remain deaf to argument. There have been instances, though—notably in the Korean war—when mere "reason" and expediency appeared to motivate Presidents. In November, 1950, after Chinese forces intervened in Korea, President Truman told a press conference that we were giving "active consideration" to "the use of the atomic bomb." In a "clarifying" statement, Mr. Truman authorized his press secretary to say, "Consideration of the use of any weapon is always implicit in the very possession of that weapon." In no time, Prime Minister Clement Attlee, of Britain— one of America's allies in Korea—announced to a cheering Parliament that he was leaving forthwith to see Mr. Truman. A few days later, a British-American communiqué dealing with numerous aspects of the war included this paragraph: "The President stated that it was his hope that world conditions would never call for the use of the atomic bomb. The President told the Prime Minister that it was also his desire to keep the Prime Minister at all times informed of developments which might bring about a change in the situation."

President Eisenhower made it plain in his memoirs that he did not regard possible use of the bomb with "ritualistic abhorrence." He recalled that upon being asked at a press conference whether the United States would use tactical atomic weapons in a general war in

Asia, he replied, "Against a strictly military target, the answer would be yes." Later, speaking broadly on the same subject, he told a reporter that he knew only two things about war: "The most unpredictable factor in war was human nature, but the only unchanging factor in war was human nature. . . . And the next thing is that every war is going to astonish you in the way it occurred, and in the way it is carried out." Contemplating the outbreak of a general Asian war, he wrote, "It was clear that we would have to use atomic weapons." Another entry tells of a meeting with Prime Minister Churchill in Bermuda in 1953: "The only part of the discussion that led to definite opposition from Winston was our announcement that in the event of renewed attack [by the Chinese in Korea] we would feel free to use the atomic bomb against military targets, whenever military advantages dictated such use. This awakened in Winston many fears. Britain, he argued, was a small crowded island; one good nuclear bombing could destroy it, and recklessness might provoke such a catastrophe. I earnestly assured Winston that I had no intention of acting rashly, saying that I merely wanted our friends to know that past limitations on our actions . . . would not necessarily be observed."

Richard Nixon, while campaigning for office in 1968, spoke with approbation of President Eisenhower's desire to let friendly powers know how seriously America took the Korean war. A similar approach might work for the Vietnam war, Nixon implied. Talking to Southern delegates at the Republican Convention, in Miami Beach, he said, "How do you bring a war to a conclusion? I'll tell you how Korea was ended. We got in there and had this messy war on our hands. Eisenhower let the word go out—let the word go out diplomatically—to the Chinese and the North Koreans that we would not tolerate this continual ground war of attrition. And within a matter of months they negotiated." In March, 1955, while he was Vice-President, Mr. Nixon told the Executive Club of Chicago, "The weapons which were used during the

Korean war and World War Two are obsolete. Our artillery and our tactical Air Force in the Pacific are now equipped with atomic explosives which can and will be used on military targets with precision and effectiveness. It is foolish to talk about the possibility that the weapons which might be used in the event war breaks out in the Pacific would be limited to the conventional Korean and World War Two types of explosives. Our forces could not fight an effective war in the Pacific with those types of explosives if they wanted to. Tactical atomic explosives are now conventional and will be used against the military targets of any aggressive force."

If a President did decide to launch a nuclear warhead against Vietnam—or anywhere else—he would not lack willing hands to carry out his orders. This was the unsurprising impression I gained while wandering through the Pentagon, whose labyrinthine corridors led me to the offices of various military spokesmen. None of these men bluntly urged the use of nuclear bombs in the Vietnam war, but a number of them had a good deal to say about our failure to do so in the Korean war when hordes of Chinese troops were crossing the Yalu River—a time, it will be recalled, when Russia loved China but wasn't nearly the nuclear power it has since become. In addition to representing a missed opportunity, it was asserted, the Korean war had probably conditioned us to think of atomic bombs as forbidden armament—an effect whose importance, it was said, may have transcended that of the war itself. One civilian official told me, "If the Chinese invaded Vietnam the way they did Korea, it would be a national disgrace if we didn't clobber them with nukes. And another thing—this time the Russians wouldn't mind it."

In the Pentagon, I listened to considerable talk about "tactical" nuclear weapons—weapons, it was stressed, that were not to be confused with "strategic" ones, in general America's highest-yield systems, which were usually denounced there as monstrous city-killers. Compared to them, I gathered from Defense Department people, tacticals bordered on the humane, since, in theory, their use would be confined to military targets; thousands of tacticals had been stored for years in South Korea, Guam, Okinawa, and other Far Eastern points within easy delivery distance of Indo-China. In contrast to most strategic weapons, whose explosive yields range from hundreds of thousands to millions of tons of TNT, tacticals start at tens of tons and go on up to many times the twenty-thousand-ton yield that obliterated Hiroshima. An ordnance analyst who discussed tacticals with me said that if he were President and we were losing a war he would not have the slightest hesitation about availing himself of tacticals. "In a way, they're middle-of-the-road weapons—more powerful than conventional ones but not as devastating as strategics," he told me. He added parenthetically that he was generalizing, without reference to Vietnam.

Both in and out of the Pentagon, I found, tacticals were a rife topic, the interest in them turning on whether their utility offered a specious excuse for "crossing the nuclear threshold." People who had misgivings about them argued that the lower a weapon's yield, the more thinkable its use. Ambassador Vance told me, "Those who see merit in tacticals claim that they are nothing but large explosives whose use would result in limited casualties and limited contamination. I consider that a fantasy, and, fortunately, I believe that is also the view of many Soviet leaders. In my opinion, if tacticals were used, there would be retaliation in kind, and before very long strategics would be in the picture." A man who had been Assistant Secretary of Defense in the Johnson Administration told me, "I would destroy tacticals. Strategics are worth having. They keep both us and the Russians well behaved." He also said that the reputedly low yields of tacticals had a way of filling some people's heads with gimmicky notions; one such notion he had heard of was the fashioning of a nuclear hand grenade, its power to be the equivalent of five thousand tons of TNT—which, he recalled, "used to be a good night's yield over Berlin in World War Two." To a disarmament scholar at the Brookings Institution, however, the line of demarcation between tacticals and strategics was very much in the eye of the beholder. In practice, he told me, the likeliest use of tacticals would be to defend friendly soil, and thus, if Russion forces invaded West Germany, we, in keeping with NATO agreements, might throw tacticals at the invaders The Germans, surveying the damage to themselves and their homeland, might easily feel that they had been defended by weapons that were more strategic than tactical. "One nation's tactical may well be another's strategic," the scholar remarked.

In 1970, the proponents of tacticals saw little chance of having their way in the immediate future. Of the Vietnam war, a Pentagon official said, "Winning it with nukes is out." He spoke bleakly of his government's policy of non-victory, but then so did his colleagues, all of whom insisted that the military had fallen low in public esteem. A Defense physicist blamed this on the public's "emotional attitude" toward nuclear weapons. He was confident, however, that before too long the military would regain its good name. "I have faith in Americans," the physicist said. "We thrive on crises. That's when we're at our best. Take Cuba. Take the Sputnik. Look at how we rose to those crises. And if one comes along in Vietnam we'll do just as well."

In the absence of any such crisis, United States forces persevered in Vietnam with conventional arms, secure in the knowledge that their government's atomic bombs could spare the country from total defeat. They represented America's supreme military option, but, from everything I could learn, it was not clear whether they were a guarantee against defeat or against victory. In Washington, I found little interest in resolving this

dilemma, with the minds of governmental leaders fixed
on keeping their formidable option open, blurred though
it might be. It was a familiar approach, its ends pursued
with familiar means. The ultimate weapon continued to
be made more ultimate, in the United States and, no
doubt, in Russia; in the Pentagon I heard enthusiastic
reports of improved accuracy in American missiles. The
guessing game of "enoughness" went on unabated, its
premise being "We must not have too many nukes or the
enemy will feel threatened, but we must not have too few
or he will attack." Contingency plans proliferated, their
chief producer the Joint Chiefs of Staff, the Pentagon's
highest echelon. The Joint Chiefs were charged by the
National Security Act with giving the President the
benefit of their professional experience, but since there
were no veterans of full-scale nuclear exchanges, the
charge may have been partly anachronistic. Having been
permitted to enter the tightly guarded precincts of the
Joint Chiefs, I sat in a Pentagon conference room with six
officers who were members of the Studies, Analysis, and
Gaming Agency, the unit that supervised war games.
These were usually played by teams of ten, I was told, the
opponents matching wits over a scenario "into which we
build a crisis." The players were "an inter-agency mix,"
and it wasn't easy to recruit them, for a game entailed two
or three sessions, each lasting hours, and, as a member of
the games unit said, "Everyone's so busy. But once they
get here, they go all out to win. They get to know each
other under pressure." He also informed me that Vietnam
war games posed special problems, saying, "It is harder
to game a limited-war complex than it is an all-out deal."
A colleague of his told me, "Something short of all-out
war seems to be the thing ahead, but that's only my
opinion. Nothing we come up with here is what you
would call 'predictive.' It's just 'probable,' with a little
'maybe' thrown in." Another of the officers said that
games sometimes allowed for the use of tacticals. When I
asked whether these involved Vietnam, he said he

preferred to remain unspecific. The same man informed me that the games depended on data regarding such factors as the enemy's system of command and control and his weapons, logistics, and established military habits. "We stick strictly to the enemy's capabilities," he told me. "We try to avoid thinking of things like intentions and public opinion."

As in the past, military requests for money continued to be made without letup. Listening to an official of a civilian agency that passed on such requests, I gathered that they were as abundant as contingency plans. The official, an old hand at his job, had the impression that the military thought the end of the world was due tomorrow. He said, "The military doesn't like to take chances, which is understandable. But putting in for any and all weapons systems just as long as they don't defy the laws of physics is something else again. It's not the way to develop great military effectiveness." Perhaps because of its preoccupation with the future, he went on, the military was sometimes slow to recognize its cultural lags. In illustration, he informed me that a lot of money had gone down the drain in Vietnam because American airmen missed their targets too often, the reason for this being that Air Force crews were in planes that had been originally designed for dropping nuclear bombs. "With nukes, a near miss is as good as a direct hit, but our pilots aren't using nukes," the official said. One of his colleagues told me that appropriations for nuclear weapons rose again in 1970—a development that pleased the Air Force. "They think nukes are their turf," he said. On Capitol Hill, though, Representative Holifield reminded me that the Navy, too, had made the nuclear scene, with its fleet of forty-one Polaris submarines, each of which had much more firepower than the United States had expended in the entire Second World War. The thought of the Polaris fleet left some Army theatre commanders unhappy, I was told by a staff investigator of the Senate Foreign Relations Committee. "A theatre commander wants control over his own bailiwick," he said. "He wants a piece of the action—meaning his own missiles. He doesn't want it on his mind that if Hanoi, or whatever, is going to be disintegrated, it'll be some invisible skipper thousands of miles away who does the job."

To sum up, there was no certainty in 1970 that America would not drop an atomic bomb on Indo-China. Indeed, there hadn't been any such certainty since at least 1966, when all the nuclear powers failed to join in support of a United Nations resolution that would have restricted the use of nuclear weapons. However, nearly all the people I interviewed regarded it as extremely unlikely that the United States would use nuclear bombs in Indo-China, their skepticism being based on their faith in the doctrine of deterence, which stands or falls on the assumption that all of us—and not least heads of state—want to live. I met no one who saw deterrence in a redemptive light; it has made long-term hostages of the populations of the United States and Russia while fostering an increasing deployment of nuclear weapons everywhere, particularly in the vicinity of Indo-China. Nevertheless, the doctrine's gospel of "No news is good news" had a lot of disciples. A reluctant one told me, "The only trouble with deterrence is that it would take just a few fools to upset it." It may be assumed, by extension, that it was no foolproof proposition that Indo-China was safe from our nuclear bombs—at least, not while the details of how the fighting would end were unknown. Mr. Rusk, among many others, hoped devoutly that it would not have a nuclear finish. "It would destroy not only the answers but the questions. It might be our last political decision," he said.

5

AWOL

🏴 🏴 🏴 🏴 🏴

Late one cloudless morning in May, 1969, Seaman Apprentice Harry Taggart (a pseudonym, like all names herein) and a Marine corporal, with whom Taggart had recently bought a used white Triumph, drove to the gate at the San Diego Naval Station, where a guard they knew dispensed with the usual formality of checking their liberty cards. He shouldn't have. Both men had leave papers, to be sure, but Taggart's were bogus. He was going AWOL. He had had his fill of military service—nearly half of a four-year enlistment. Once the guard had waved the pair on, the Marine corporal remarked, "You're really doing it, then—you're really going underground." As though in response, Taggart halted the car and got out to glare in the general direction of the big Navy base. Standing in the road beyond the camp's perimeter, though, Taggart didn't see much. All that came into view were fighter planes patrolling a pale-blue sky, the superstructures of warships riding at anchor, and, off in the distance, the vague outlines of the base's low-lying buildings. Absurdly, Taggart has since said, his eyes strained to pick out the station's brig—a squat, sand-colored building fenced in by barbed wire. He soon gave up, only mildly frustrated. He know the brig well. It wasn't long ago that he had spent two months there, subsisting on a diet that had trimmed his already slight frame by fifteen pounds. He had been jailed for going AWOL, but his escapade, he has said, had been a botch: working as a handyman at a souvenir shop in California, near Lake Tahoe, he hadn't even taken the precaution of disguising his name; at the end of seven weeks, half a dozen F.B.I. agents had come to his furnished room at four in the morning and handed him over to Navy authorities. Abruptly, Taggart broke off his presumed last look at the San Diego base and trudged back toward the Triumph. As he did so, he later recalled, he promised himself that this time he would improve on any talents he had as a fugitive from the military and its war across the Pacific.

Taggart stayed underground more than two and a half years, from 1969 to 1972, nearly all of it within American borders. The F.B.I. never did catch up with him. He turned himself in. Sustained throughout by his sentiments toward the military, he eventually yielded to the pressures of his shadowy, illegal existence, just as had thousands of other AWOLs roaming the country. It was shortly after his surrender that I met Taggart. He was then at the United States Naval Station in Brooklyn, about to be court-martialled on charges of "unauthorized absence." In was in Brooklyn that we did most of our talking, usually over an evening snack in the enlisted men's cafeteria—a dim room dominated by a strident jukebox and filled with plastic and chrome furniture; pending the outcome of his court-martial, Taggart was permitted to come and go, the same as other sailors. The subject of his trial didn't come up. He didn't raise it, and my own interest lay elsewhere. It was the life of a military runaway inside the United States that I wanted to hear

about; a noncriminal type, that is, who out of misgivings
about our policies abroad, was prepared to become an
exile at home, pitting himself against the elaborate,
ubiquitous resources of his government. Less publicized
but far more numerous than the AWOLs who had chosen
to settle in Canada, Sweden, and other foreign countries,
these domestic refugees were exceedingly elusive; unlike
expatriate deserters, they could not reveal who they were
without facing instant arrest.

I was put on to Taggart by a Philadelphia woman I
know who was active in the peace movement and who
had helped him at a turning point in the course of his long
flight. She told me little about Taggart other than that he
had no politics to speak of and that he was willing to see
me. She warned me that underground AWOLs were
generally difficult to talk with and that Taggart, who had
been on the run longer than most, was no exception. She
proved to be right. A short, brown-eyed man of
twenty-three who looked seventeen and who bore a
disconcerting resemblance to Stan Laurel, Taggart more
often than not received my questions with wariness, his
answers terse, his manner hard and faintly condescend-
ing. After some of my talks with him, I could look back on
nothing more than ten or fifteen minutes of grudging,
desultory conversation. At his most expansive, Taggart
was good for perhaps an hour, after which, his eyes
narrowing shrewdly, his face would once again assume
its familiar frozen mask of suspicion. Nevertheless,
Taggart persevered with our talks, gradually and pains-
takingly piecing together the details of his fugitive years.
He never explained his doggedness. I myself thought he
very much wanted to hear himself recall the events of his
driven, precarious odyssey; I thought he wanted to
convince himself, now that it was over, that he had
actually lived it.

Taggart and the Marine corporal, Ray Hume, left the
base and moved north along the coast, bound first for

Taggart's home, in Denver, and then east for Hume's, in
Syracuse. They were on the road five days, and in the
many silences he shared with his companion, Taggart has
said, his thoughts rarely strayed from the step he was
taking. They certainly didn't, he said, when, two hours
out of San Diego, road signs announced that they were
nearing Pasadena. Taggart knew it as the home of the
California Institute of Technology. He had been at the
Institute the previous week, he told me, to confer with an
instructor about his plans for going AWOL; a fellow-pris-
oner in the brig, a Quaker who often spoke of an
"underground railway," had given Taggart the instructor's name. The teacher's advice had been to "go north,"
meaning to Canada, and Taggart had recoiled from the
idea. "I wanted no part of it," he told me. "I was
surprised by how strongly I felt about that. Until I saw
the instructor, I'd thought only about splitting—nothing
about where I'd go. But as soon as the instructor made his
suggestion, I knew it was here that I'd be AWOL. It was
my country as much as the Navy's." Taggart said he
intended no criticism of AWOLs in Canada and Sweden.
"Each AWOL has to do things his own way," he said.
And each AWOL, he added, had his own motives,
including some that Taggart considered foolish; in the
brig, he said, he had met a sailor who was there because
he had gone home to ride his motorbike.

Discussing his own disaffection in some detail, Taggart
said that it went back to the day of his enlistment, in June,
1967. Just turned eighteen and newly graduated from
high school, he said, he had presented himself at a Navy
recruiting station in downtown Denver, his sole motive
the prospect of adventure. He knew nothing of politics.
He didn't read newspapers. His religious training was nil,
his parents being lapsed Presbyterians. All that explained
his presence at the recruiting office, he said, was an
intense desire to serve with an underwater-demolition
team, one of the Navy's most hazardous assignments. "I
love being underwater," Taggart told me. "I've scuba-
dived since I was twelve. If I was going to be in the Navy,

I wanted excitement. The recruiting officer said yes, yes, yes, I could be a frogman. It was a very big deal to me. I didn't know then that he was just a salesman. I mistook him for Uncle Sam. I signed up for four years." But Taggart was doomed to disappointment. After taking his basic training at San Diego, he was sent to the Advanced Undersea Weapons School, at Key West, Florida, where he was told that he was being prepared for submarine service. Outraged, Taggart reminded his superiors that he had been assured of underwater-demolition duty. For his trouble, he was sent to sea as a clerk aboard the *Shangri-La*, an aircraft carrier that was gone about a year on a tour of European ports. Taggart was too angry, though, to notice the Continent. His every thought was given to being with an underwater team in Vietnam. He filled out innumerable forms to that effect, all of which were carefully pigeonholed by his division chief. "It seemed I was a good clerk," Taggart told me. "The whole business was wild—I was being punished with a desk job for wanting hazardous duty in Vietnam." He went over his division chief's head, taking up the question of his transfer with high-ranking officers. They turned him down, and he grew insolent toward them—for which he was restricted to quarters. "The time was past for being nice," Taggart told me. "A year and a half had gone by, and the government was still welshing on its contract." When the *Shangri-La* completed its mission, docking at Jacksonville, Florida, Taggart took off on the abortive flight that ended up in the San Diego brig. He had already told me about that, Taggart recalled, but he hadn't told me that directly after his emergence from the brig, early in 1969, he had spent some time driving Marines from the base to Camp Pendleton, fifty minutes away—a training area for troops who would soon go to Vietnam. His passengers, he said, had all been there before and had volunteered for a second round of fighting. To a man, Taggart told me, they were gung ho about the opportunity, their talk charged with an eagerness to repeat experiences they had already had—killing Vietnamese, raping their wives, using children for target practice, "wasting" prisoners of war. Listening to the Marines, Taggart said, he felt foolish for having aspired to be a frogman in Vietnam. "If it didn't kill me, it would leave me sounding like those Marines," he said. The thought sealed his discontent, helping him overcome a hesitation at going AWOL a second time, which, as he pointed out, could entail the loss of G.I. benefits and a year or more at hard labor. Taggart said, "Those Marines convinced me that the government had been taking me, in more ways than one. The same went for the Marines themselves, but I wasn't thinking of them when I made my decision."

The afternoon of their second day on the road, Taggart and Hume arrived at the Taggart residence, a modest, comfortable frame house. Taggart hadn't notified his parents of his arrival, but since it was a Sunday—a warm, still one—he know they would be taking it easy in their living room; his father worked as a printer, and his mother part time as a hairdresser in a department store. He had in mind only a brief visit—no more than a few hours. It was Syracuse, Hume's city, that was Taggart's true destination, for it was there that he planned to take up his new life. Nothing, though, could have kept him from going home, he said. He had no idea when he might again be able to see his parents or a brother, a year older than he was, who was at Fort Benning, Georgia, training with a Green Beret unit. As Taggart expected, his parents welcomed him and his friend. His father shook hands warmly with Hume, and his mother insisted that the young men stay for for dinner. Taggart had no intention of informing his parents that he was going AWOL. It would only upset them, he told me, and, besides, they were constitutionally incapable of lying or concealment; if F.B.I. agents were to ask them questions about their son, they would tell whatever they knew. As a result, he sat taciturn in the living room. "I felt as though I were both visiting and avoiding my parents," Taggart told me.

Twenty minutes before dinner, he picked up a seabag with which he had arrived and went to his room. It was crowded with mementos of his premilitary past—a high-school pennant, scuba-diving equipment, a picture of himself competing in a swimming meet, another that showed him and his brother singing with a Y glee club. The seabag, Taggart said, was filled with Navy clothing, and now, undressing, he added the uniform he was wearing to its contents. Knotting the seabag, he stowed it in the darkest corner of his closet. He then bathed, and when he reappeared in the living room he had on a blue serge suit—the one in which he had graduated from high school. His parents and Hume stared at him in silence. "No one was fooling no one," Taggart told me. His parents didn't comment on his change of clothes, but at dinner Mr. Taggart, speaking broadly, said that sometimes young people made mistakes that lasted a lifetime; flouting one's obligations to the government, he said, could be one of those mistakes. At the door, as the two young men were leaving, Mrs. Taggart asked her son, in a doubtful voice, to keep in touch. It was dark when he and Hume were back in their car, and Taggart took the wheel. "I drove fast," he said. "I wanted to see what I had let myself in for."

In Syracuse, Hume introduced Taggart to his friends. "I named myself Mark West," Taggart told me. Hume's friends made up a widely assorted group, among them students and instructors at colleges in the Syracuse area. For the most part, they were nonpolitical, like Hume himself, but two or three were peace activists. Eventually, Taggart said, he made friends of his own, but, for getting started in a strange town, he could hardly have hoped for a better sponsor than Hume. By the time the Marine returned to duty in San Diego, after a leave of six weeks, Taggart had a girl, a job, and a home. He and the girl, Marie Pinto, were together whenever they could be, which wasn't always, since she was a sophomore at a small college for girls thirty miles north of Syracuse, where she was taking summer courses. As for the job, it wasn't much—a temporary one as a parking-lot attendant, for which he was paid at the end of each day. His home was a well-furnished five-room house in a quiet, middle-class neighborhood. Taggart shared the house with four other young bachelors, and among them, he said, they had no difficulty in meeting the monthly rental, of two hundred and sixty dollars. Taggart's co-tenants were a hulking snowmobile salesman with a drinking problem; a railroad clerk; a would-be sculptor with an independent income; and a premed student at Syracuse University, who worked evenings in a pharmacy around the corner. The house was the scene of many parties, Taggart told me, but its occupants didn't get along. "There was no telling who'd fly off the handle next," he said. "They appointed me general peacemaker, and I was kept busy." Despite their volatility, Taggart entrusted them with the secret of his illegal status. He did it reluctantly, holding off until what he considered the last minute—just short of three months after he had left San Diego. By that time, Taggart said, he judged that the F.B.I. was surely on his trail. According to him, the Navy gave its AWOLs several weeks in which to come back on their own; if they didn't, the military, classifying these runaways as deserters, called in the F.B.I., which required additional time for processing records, some of which were stored in its mammoth memory bank in Washington. Taggart said, "I asked the guys in the house to stall any cops who might come looking for an AWOL. I asked them to let me know the minute that happened, no matter where I was, so that I could get some kind of head start. Each of them gave me his word that he'd do exactly what I asked. There wasn't anything else I could do. I was in their hands."

Once Taggart had faced the daily threat posed by the F.B.I., he took steps to meet it. Just naming himself Mark West wasn't enough. The pseudonym, Taggart told me, had to be fleshed out, so to speak, with a Social Security number, credit cards, and other such trappings. "The more I acquired a new identity, the tougher the F.B.I.'s job would be," Taggart said. Further complicating the government's hunt, he went on, was the increasing number of AWOL cases, the press of which, he said, had the F.B.I.'s limited manpower scrambling in all directions. The increase in AWOL cases was also a boon to his morale. "It was lonely being an AWOL, but I knew I wasn't alone," he said. "If I hadn't known I was one of many doing the same thing about the war, I could have thought of myself as leading the life of an ordinary thief." Another incentive for Taggart's establishing a new identity was that it would enable him to look around for better employment; unlike most employers, the parking-lot owner, who impressed him as a fly-by-nighter, hadn't even asked him whether he had a Social Security card. "I wasn't earning enough," Taggart said. "I wanted to buy Marie an engagement ring." With the aid of the peace activists he had met through Hume, Taggart became a card-carrying nonentity. The activists, he said, put him in touch with two AWOLs, from whom he learned that there were techniques for documenting oneself. In his case, Taggart told me, the crucial document proved anticlimactically easy to come by. This was a new draft card, and he got it, he said, when the AWOLs produced not one but two blank cards, one of which Taggart filled out in the name of Mark West. He was advised to keep the other in reserve. "The AWOLs said that in an emergency I might need it," Taggart told me. "I asked no questions. I figured the cards were stolen—maybe in a raid on draft offices somewhere." Armed with a draft card, Taggart continued, he had no trouble getting a driver's license; nor was there any difficulty in obtaining a Social Security card. One simply applied for it, using a fake return address; the AWOLs, Taggart said, told him of an apartment building that had several empty mailboxes. With these credentials, Taggart qualified for a number of credit cards and a library card. He also became a clubman, it being a mere

formality to join organizations such as the Young
Republicans and the Y.M.C.A. The list of affiliations went
on and on, Taggart said, until his wallet bulged with
twenty cards, all attesting to the existence of Mark West.

Vested with the respectability of his documents,
Taggart sought a new job, and in a week or so he was
taken on as a riveter in a small sheet-metal factory. He
earned a hundred and ten dollars a week—considerably
more than he had been paid at the parking lot. In
addition, Taggart said, he worked overtime whenever he
could, putting aside money for Marie's ring and a used
car for himself. (Hume had bought out Taggart's share in
the Triumph.) For the first ten days, Taggart recalled, he
was on tryout, his boss, an intense middle-aged Pole,
closely watching his every move. Taggart, though, was
doing a little counter-watching, he told me, trying to
decide whether his employer was the kind of man to
whom he could reveal the fact of his outlaw status. If he
couldn't do that, Taggart had decided, he wouldn't take
the job. "It wouldn't be fair, deceiving the boss," he told
me. "He had to know that I might be picked up any day
and he'd suddenly be short a riveter. Except for one job, I
did that with all my employers. Naturally, I'd first size
each of them up. If he tipped his attitude toward the war,
it would be easy to know what to do. Mostly, though, all
that I had to go by was the sound of his voice and the look
in his eye." At the sheet-metal factory, Taggart said, the
disclosure of his deserter status, when he made it, was
taken in stride. His employer, he said, turned over the
news a moment, then shrugged and said, "You work hard
and your hair is short. In the factory, we don't make
politics."

In two months' time, Taggart presented Marie with a
three-hundred-dollar ring; she was nineteen and he
nearly twenty-one. Ten days later, toward the end of
September, the two flew to Denver for a weekend with
Taggart's parents. Taggart made the trip apprehensively,
he said; an AWOL he knew had recently been arrested

while attending his sister's funeral. Marie and his parents took to each other at once, Taggart said, but the weekend wasn't all smooth. Calling on a boyhood friend who lived a few doors away, Taggart learned that a couple of months before the F.B.I. had been up and down the street inquiring about him. According to the friend, agents had questioned Mr. and Mrs. Taggart, informing them that their son might be shot on sight, because he was "armed and dangerous." Taggart thought of apologizing to his parents, he told me, but, curiously, he couldn't bring himself to do it. "My being AWOL was something that was out in the world, beyond the family," he said. IIis parents said nothing about the agents' interview, either. In contrast to his last visit home, Taggart went on, his father now expressed uncertainty about the government's course in Indo-China. Taggart attributed the change in his father's tone to the fact that news of American atrocities and drug addiction in Asia had only recently come to light. As he and Marie were leaving, Taggart said, he noticed that this time his mother didn't ask him to keep in touch. "She must have realized that it could lead to my arrest," he said. In point of fact, Taggart told me, he did keep in touch, writing general news of himself. His letters, though, bore misleading postmarks, to throw police off his trail. His correspondence home, he said, was mailed by friends living in places far from wherever he himself happened to be. Throughout his underground years, Taggart told me, he heard nothing from his parents or his brother, his whereabouts as much a mystery to them as to the police.

Back in Syracuse, Taggart pursued his routine at the sheet-metal factory, his employer continuing to treat him the same as he had before learning Taggart's secret. The plant was doing well, Taggart said—particularly right after he and Marie returned from Denver. In this period, he told me, there was frequent need for his overtime services, and that was fortunate, since Marie was busy studying for exams. Evenings, he said, he wouldn't get home until nine or ten, and then he would make himself a sandwich, chat a while with whoever was around the house, and turn in. One evening, though, a cold one in late October, when he wasn't riveting overtime, Taggart came home early enough to sniff the aroma of a meal in preparation. The snowmobile salesman—Hank Dorn— and a girl friend were eating in. "Roast beef—join us," Dorn said by way of greeting. He reeked of bourbon, and his eyes, bloodshot, were out of focus. Listing slightly, he disappeared in the direction of his room. Taggart remained in the kitchen with Dorn's friend, whom he had met before. She was a quiet, well-spoken girl, he told me, the daughter of a high administrative official at Cornell University. Taggart was helping her with the meal when Dorn reappeared, his hair dishevelled and one shoe missing. He stood in the center of the kitchen, towering over the girl and Taggart, swaying, uncertain what to do. He looked blankly from the girl to Taggart, and then, raising his voice, directed a stream of abuse at her, accusing her of making passes at Taggart. The girl began to weep, and Dorn kept up his tirade. Taggart said, "I told him to stop being mouthy. He took a step toward me and I backed up. I didn't want to hurt him. I knew karate." Blubbering with rage, Dorn suddenly shouted, "I'm going to the drugstore." He did exactly that, as Taggart later found out from the premed student who worked there. The student reported that Dorn, using a public phone, had spilled all to the police—Taggart's AWOL status, where he could be found that minute, the address of the sheet-metal factory. What Taggart found out for himself, he told me, was that five minutes after Dorn had fled the house a police car approached, its siren low, its dome light flashing. Taggart didn't take long to act. Without pausing to grab up anything he owned, he dashed, coatless, into the back yard and clambered over a fence, dropping into a neighbor's garden. There he burst through a neatly clipped hedge and into another neighbor's garden, where a growling boxer chased after him. Barely escaping the dog, Taggart kept going in the cold, garden after garden, his steeplechase leading him to a bus route and freedom of a sort. Halting to catch his breath in one of the yards, he made up his mind he would get even with his betrayer. "I swore that if I ever saw Dorn again, I'd use karate, even if he was blind drunk," Taggart said.

Taggart hid out in Marie's dorm. He lived there with her and forty-nine other girls for two months. Like the other dormitories at the girls' college, Marie's had a housemother, whose presence, one gathers from the school catalogue, was calculated to keep the girls in line as well as to afford them "the wisdom of a woman of mature years." In harboring him, Taggart told me, Marie ran the danger of expulsion, which bothered him, since he had been brought up to think highly of a college education; he had hoped to gain one himself through the G.I. Bill. Fortunately, Taggart said, he was able to retrieve his belongings after phoning the premed student, who delivered them to the dorm. The student also brought tidings, which he passed on to Taggart in the visitors' lounge: The week after Taggart left, police had come to the house and quizzed Dorn and the others about Taggart's whereabouts; Dorn had moved out of the house at the request of its three other occupants; to celebrate his departure, the three had gone on a drinking spree, for which they, in turn, had been evicted. "Any room here?" Taggart's former co-tenant asked, looking around the comfortable, carpeted lounge. Taggart shook his head. Undiscouraged, the student said, "Maybe you can get me a date some night. I'll phone you." Taggart replied, "That wouldn't be cool."

For Taggart, life in his bizarre sanctuary was seldom routine. Unexpected situations might arise at any time. Fire drills, for instance. They might be planned surprises for the girls, but for Taggart they were cliff-hangers. When the gongs went off, sometimes in the dead of night, he said, campus guards would comb the dorm, checking

each room for malingerers. "It was hairy," Taggart
recalled. "I'd be in Marie's closet, crouched in a corner
behind her dresses. I wouldn't breathe until the footsteps
went away." Cleaning women were also a problem. All of
them, in Taggart's estimation, were ignorant biddies
—there would have been no pleading with them if they
had discovered that a male was within the gates. On two
occasions, Taggart said, when Marie was at classes,
cleaning women perfunctorily rapped on her door,
preparatory to entering; in his best falsetto, Taggart told
them to come back later. Mornings, the domestics had an
interminable coffee break in the dorm lobby, blocking
Taggart's exit from the building. One day, aching for a
walk and unwilling to wait out their social hour, he left
by descending an outdoor fire escape. Halfway down, he
found himself staring straight at the housemother,
coming along a path. Taggart wasn't fazed. Unlike the
cleaning women, she was no threat. "You naughty boy, I
didn't see you," the housemother told him as his feet
touched the ground. Taggart was accustomed to her
indulgences, he informed me. A middle-aged widow with
red dyed hair and rhinestone-rimmed glasses, she
preferred Taggart to any of the other young men who
called on the girls in her care. The reason was simple:
Taggart fussed over her. When a bridge game was
organized, he said, he would insist on being her partner,
claiming that he and the housemother made a perfect
team. Taggart was certain that she knew what was up but
had chosen to wink at it. Evidence clearly pointed in this
direction. For example, Taggart said, she never com-
plained to Marie that he ate daily at the dorm; other
young men had meals there, too, but only occasionally.
Citing another example, Taggart told me that in his
second month at the dorm he and the housemother found
themselves as guests at a late-evening birthday party in
one of the girls' rooms. "No men allowed in dorm rooms,"
she admonished Taggart, and then, reconsidering, she

shook her finger coquettishly and said, "Well, just this once."

The girls themselves, Taggart went on, seemed undisturbed by his presence, which, he said, didn't necessarily mean that it sat well with all of them. Perhaps Marie's popularity explained his apparent acceptance, he conjectured, or perhaps his care and feeding impressed the girls as a kind of extracurricular project. In any event, he said, he was never made to feel anything but welcome, the girls seeming determined to greet him at all times. Even when he was showering, Taggart said, one of them was likely to call out, "How are things going, Harry?" All the girls knew him by his real name. Marie wouldn't have it any other way. "It wouldn't be honest," she maintained. As far as he knew, Taggart said, the girls kept his identity a house secret—which, in retrospect, seemed remarkable, since they were products of genteel, conservative homes. Like Marie, the other had little interest in politics; they were concerned only with giving refuge to someone who needed it. "They were like sisters to me," Taggart said.

Notwithstanding the girls' hospitality, Taggart continued, life in the dorm wasn't easy. He didn't know what to do with his time. Each day, he said, the hours stretched ahead like a trackless desert. He lacked the patience to read. He resented his good health. "The way I was living, I should have been an invalid," he said. "Day in and day out, I'd sit at Marie's window, watching the campus. After a certain point, I wasn't just bored, I was depressed. I didn't know what I was waiting for. Even if the war ended, I'd still be in trouble." Conscious of his low spirits, Marie did what she could. If there was a long enough break between classes, she would come back to her room and be with him awhile. She persuaded the one girl in the dorm with a television set—sets were forbidden—to let Taggart use it weekdays. It proved to be a companion of sorts. Several specials had to do with events in Asia. One program he saw showed small

Vietnamese boys selling heroin to American troops in
Saigon. Another described American atrocities, confirming the stories he had first heard from the Vietnam-bound
Marines in California. "There seemed to be nothing that
was right about the war and plenty that was wrong," he
said. Taggart had no illusions about his being a martyr, he
told me, but he vaguely began to suspect that in going
AWOL he might have done something more important
than he had realized.

The longer Taggart stayed on in the dorm the more
restless he grew, his itch to light out for somewhere
intensified by the approach of his twenty-first birthday.
All his brooding, he said, wasn't helping him figure out a
fresh course of action, which he recognized as his
immediate need. One night, he told Marie he had to go
away to get his bearings, and in an hour or two the word
was out that the dorm was about to lose its man. Over the
next few days, he recalled, many of the girls gave him
snapshots of themselves, inscribed "To Harry." Taggart
discarded the keepsakes. Outside the dorm, he explained
to me, they might provide the police with a clue to his
identity. He said, "If I were in an accident, or maybe a
fight, those snaps would be on me along with my phony
papers." Two nights before he left, Marie casually
suggested that they drop in on a girl who lived in a suite
down the hall. When they did, Taggart could barely
squeeze into the place. Two dozen girls, some of them in
pajamas, were waiting for him. It was his birthday, and
they had laid on a surprise party, complete with cake and
candles. The festivities included a gift—a toy lion of
orange rubber. Its presentation by one of the girls was
marked by a brief toast: "From all of us to the lion of our
dorm."

Taggart moved fast after leaving Marie's school.
Proceeding to Syracuse, he spent the night at the home of
one of the activists who had helped him with his
documents. The next day, he was on his way to Montreal,
one of three AWOLs in a dilapidated car—a part of "the

railway"—driven by a minister in his early forties. "I wasn't going to Canada to stay," Taggart told me. "I just wanted to get my head together." In Montreal, he was put up temporarily by two Syracusans, both "railway" agents. Since he wasn't bilingual, his job pickings were slim. He did, however, manage to find an opening as janitor of a small office building, which paid enough to meet his few needs. He was in Canada a good part of the winter of 1970, and, increasingly, he grew aware of a state of drift on his part. "I had no control over things," he explained. "They just seemed to happen to me. Maybe it had been that way in Syracuse, too, but now it was spelled out."

In Montreal, he fell in socially with an extremist group composed of American deserters and Canadians who were for French separatism in Quebec Province. Weekly, he said, they practiced guerrilla warfare in a wooden section on the outskirts of the city, tossing Molotov cocktails and assembling weapons, which they fired at targets. Taggart joined the extremists at these sessions, and also at classes in advanced karate, judo, and jujitsu. It was an odd experience, he said, for he was opposed to violent politics and yet he was drawn to the group's violent rehearsals. "Why was that?" he asked rhetorically. "It was something to guard against." Another thing that happened to him involved a private detective. He first spied the man standing by a disabled convertible on the side of a highway. Taggart, who was driving along in a borrowed car, pulled over to see whether he could help. In ten minutes, he had the convertible in working order, and the grateful motorist invited Taggart to follow him to a well-known bar. The two got along famously, and by the time drinks were over Taggart was in luck. "He offered me a job at twice what I was making and asked me to share his apartment, rent-free," he said. Taggart gladly accepted, and spent the better part of a month helping the detective track down assorted adulterers and shady building contractors. As a result, he said, he learned how to tail cars unobtrusively, use telephoto lenses, and eavesdrop electronically. Taggart said it wasn't lost on

him as an AWOL that this know-how might come in
handy when he returned to the States. "With what I
picked up in Montreal, I began to think I could stay
underground forever," he remarked.

Taggart spent most of his Canadian sojourn in Toronto.
Hundreds of deserters and draft dodgers were living
there, and their concentrated numbers, Taggart said, gave
him the sensation that the entire underground had
surfaced. The effect was confusing and far from
reassuring, for in the main, it seemed to him, the exiles
formed a rootless colony, their future as shapeless as their
present. Many of them were admirable people, he said,
but their ranks, like those of active servicemen, also
included drug addicts and, preponderantly, the destitute.
Thieving was common among them, usually from each
other. Their work habits were fitful, even when they
could find jobs, which were in short supply. Scores of
girls had followed their young men to Canada, he said,
many of them as wives; he remembered seeing couples
with infants wandering aimlessly in snowstorms. In
particular, Taggart told me, he found it hard to identify
with AWOLs who were being coached by physicians to
feign catatonic states and other psychiatric symptoms,
with the idea of going back to the States and receiving
medical discharges. Taggart felt a superiority over these
men, he told me. He was pleased, he said, that he had
volunteered for hazardous duty overseas, even though his
assignment hadn't come through.

Compared with other exiles, Taggart did well while he
was in Toronto, landing a job as a computer researcher at
the University of Toronto. It paid him a hundred dollars a
week—a salary that enabled him to rent a comfortably
furnished apartment near the school. He enrolled in two
humanities courses there, neither of them for credit. "I
studied hard," he said. "I though I'd lost the knack for
that." Taggart also made friends with faculty members,
who entertained him socially. One of them, an anti-war
activist of long standing, advised him to settle in

Philadelphia when he reentered the States; that city, she said, had a sensible, well-disciplined peace movement. As though to cap the nice setup he seemed to have going, Marie arrived. Unfortunately, though, she brought problems. A wealthy uncle of hers had died, leaving her a considerable legacy, and she had come to Canada to tell Taggart that she believed the time was ripe for them to get married. But there was a hitch: Marie was certain that her parents wouldn't hear of having a deserter as a son-in-law. Taggart told me, "Marie wanted me to give myself up and take my punishment, after which we'd marry without any hassle. I said I'd think it over. I was stalling. Not that I didn't care for Marie. But I wanted to have something to show for all the time I'd put in as an AWOL. I had no idea what it was, but I just wasn't ready to turn myself in. Marie hung around a couple of days, then went back to Syracuse, with everything between us up in the air."

In Toronto, Taggart busied himself with affairs of the exiles' community—an uncharacteristic display of social consciousness that took various forms. One of them was to put up newly arrived AWOLs in his apartment, but this hospitable impulse, he said, was short-lived. "Whenever I came home, the fridge was cleaned out," he told me. "One guy left me stuck with a fifty-dollar phone bill, and another sold all my clothes while I was at my job." In his final weeks in Canada, Taggart said, he put in a good deal of time working with an organization formed by American church groups to help AWOLs and draft evaders who had crossed the border. Specifically, Taggart said, he acted as a volunteer counsellor, a post that called for him to hear out the difficulties of those who weren't faring as well as he was. They came to him for guidance, he said, but in essence the questions they asked were those that he asked himself. Where, they wanted to know, would their illegal state lead them? How would they stay afloat until they found out? Just because they didn't think of themselves as criminals, did that mean they weren't?

Whom was there to venerate? In practice, Taggart continued, such questions were obscured by immediate needs. He said, "Kids walked in off the street without a cent, maybe needing a doctor in a hurry, or not knowing where to crash for the night. But things like that could be handled. What couldn't be handled was how lost and scared they were. They talked about being deported from Canada, about getting twenty years back in the States. One guy talked about a firing squad. The look in their eyes could come only from being on the run, and that's what I was. Whether I liked it or not, I was one of them, and just thinking that made me angry with the government all over again. I could understand why guys took guerrilla training."

In extreme cases, Taggart told me, where individuals were frightened to the point of inaction, he gave them organization funds with which to phone their parents. When someone couldn't even manage that, Taggart himself got on the phone and informed the AWOL's parents that their son was in Canada and in need of their help. Almost invariably, he said, the parents came through, but now and then a mother or a father, fed up with having produced a loser, might remonstrate that the son in question was better off in Canada. When that occurred, Taggart would try to coax the parent into letting the boy come home, and advise the mother or the father to alert the AWOL's commanding officer that this was being done. Taggart said, "I'd tell parents, 'Your son needs you. He's scared and confused, like many of us up here.' I'd repeat this until, most times, the parents softened." In numerous instances, Taggart would get AWOLs started on their homeward trek by personally driving them across the border, in a car that had Canadian plates. Usually, he said, he did this when Canadians were going to a film on the American side, his car one of a long string bound for the movie house. "The border guards would wave all of us on through," he recalled. "I dressed differently each time. Sometimes I'd wear glasses. I gave my nationality as

Canadian. Once in a while, a guard would ask me for the last letter of the alphabet. It was a test. You had to say 'zed,' not 'zee,' which would have been American."

Eventually, Taggart drove himself to the American side for good. He couldn't take the Canadian scene, he said, in spite of the good job he had, his apartment, the non-credit courses; there were too many AWOLs like himself to look at each day. In the States, it appeared to him, he could feel more his own man, a loner in a scattered, invisible underground. He missed the risk of being in America, he said; without it, he had no sense of defying the government. Before he left, the university professor who had advised him to go to Philadelphia gave him the name of a friend of hers who worked with an organization called the Philadelphia Resistance. Taggart liked the name; it sounded angry, which, as he had mentioned, was how he felt. Winding up his affairs, he wrote to Marie to tell her she might be seeing him soon. He also added a couple of documents to his collection. One was a University of Toronto identification card, the other a baptismal certificate he received from a pacifist priest; it said that he had been born Lewis Larabee on August 16, 1949, in Ottawa. His last day in Toronto, Taggart said, he acquired yet another new name—Martin Hatcher—which he entered on the extra draft card he had been given in Syracuse. Before putting it in his wallet, he aged the card, sprinkling it with a couple of drops of muddy water and then, on his knees, trailing it back and forth on the ground.

When Taggart arrived in Philadelphia, he made straight for the Resistance office. The one person he knew of in the entire city was there—Kate Ramey, whose name the Toronto professor had given him. She was in her thirties, married, a mother, and an old hand at meeting AWOLs. Taggart was with her a long time, pouring forth his angry reaction to what he had seen in Canada—the half-derelict condition of compatriots, their general aimlessness, their paranoid fright of the United States government. He told Mrs. Ramey he had taken guerrilla training, and, with her organization's name in mind, let her know he was a crack marksman. When he had finished, he awaited her counsel, confident, he told me, that its tenor would match his mood. But Mrs. Ramey, he said, came up with the one piece of advice he wouldn't take: she recommended that he surrender. She told him that she wished he had come to her when he first went AWOL. At that point, she said, an organization like hers might have helped him file a petition for standing as a conscientious objector. But now it was too late. He had been gone nearly a year, Mrs. Ramey pointed out, and as long as he remained an outlaw there was little the Resistance could do in his behalf. However, she said, if he chose to lend himself to the military's judicial process, the organization would go all out for him, engaging a lawyer, appealing his case, if necessary, and keeping him in funds. There was no denying that he would be taking a gamble, she said, but, to judge by other AWOL cases, the findings against him might not be as severe as he probably anticipated; aware of how deeply the war was dividing the country, she said, the services didn't care to appear unduly punitive. But Taggart shook his head and told her, as he had told Marie, that he was determined to have something to show for all the chances he had taken as an AWOL. Otherwise, he said, it would seem as though he had done himself and his future no good. Taggart said, "I tried to get Kate to see that it was the closest I could come to winning out over the government. I told her that if I went to jail now I'd leave it with zero to look back on and zero ahead. Kate acted as though she had heard it all before, then gave me an address where I could have a bed."

Taggart spent the night in the home of a mathematics professor. It was on a campus, Taggart told me, and it afforded him considerably more than a bed, for on walking into the professor's house he found himself enfolded in the warmth of a harmonious family of parents and three tractable children. It was the dinner hour, Taggart recalled, and he sat down to the best meal he had had in many weeks. Afterward, alone with the professor in his study, Taggart again spoke about Canada, and at the conclusion of his account, he said, the professor remarked that it seemed edged with an approbation of violence. When Taggart remained silent, the professor said that there was a case to be made for change through violence but that he didn't see it. He spoke of the indivisibility of means and ends. He said it would be a sellout for the peace movement to ape the government's reliance on the use of force; besides, he added, that would lead only to counterforce, and plenty of it. Taggart said to me, "He wasn't telling me anything new, but I needed to hear it. It was what I myself believed. I must have been drifting away from it." When the two men, one twice the age of the other, came out of the study, the professor's wife invited Taggart to live with her family. She and her husband showed him upstairs to a large, comfortable room, then left. Alone, Taggart told me, he stared out of a dormer window at the campus below, tree-lined and dark; he felt pleased with himself, he said, for having studied in Toronto. He doubted, though, that he would soon be sitting in a classroom again. Taggart said, "I was back in America, and my mind was going to have to stay busy along different lines."

Through Mrs. Ramey and other members of the Resistance, Taggart told me, he came to know more university teachers, and also some physicians, scientists, and other professionals, several of whom, like the math professor, offered him spare rooms. Taggart was in Philadelphia nearly four months, and in all that time he had no need to rent a place of his own. "I had four homes I could sleep in, and I used them all," he said. "I'd pick the one nearest to where I happened to be." None of the people he met, he said, tried to sell him on any doctrinaire approach to politics; indeed, they frequently disagreed among themselves. There were no differences, though,

Taggart said, when it came to opposing the war, and, apparently, he added, the organization did it effectively, since the F.B.I. kept close tabs on its activities. While he was in Philadelphia, Taggart said, he frequently heard that the agency was bugging the phones of anti-war groups throughout the area; this close surveillance, Taggart said, followed several raids on local draft offices, which preceded, by a year, the highly publicized theft of records from the F.B.I. office in Media, a Philadelphia suburb. Taggart himself was tailed late one night when he left a Resistance party. Thanks to techniques he had learned in Montreal, he told me, he was able to shake his pursuer after a dozen blocks. Taggart said, "I didn't know anything the F.B.I. wanted to know, but, still, it was a close call. They could have had me as an AWOL." Taggart steered clear of political activities, his anti-war friends pointing out that the risks he would run far exceeded their own. It was especially impressed on him that he should avoid demonstrations, which were regarded as gathering grounds for F.B.I. agents posing as spectators and photographers. As a kind of self-dare, however, Taggart did attend a huge outdoor rally protesting the invasion of Cambodia in April, 1970. Standing at the edge of the crowd, he told me, he listened to a series of speakers, whose impassioned rhetoric left him cold. "It didn't seem to have anything to do with me," Taggart said. "Living underground, the way I was, all that counted was keeping out of the brig from one day to the next."

As soon as Taggart was settled in Philadelphia, he left to spend a weekend with Marie. In the months since she had been to Toronto, she had transferred to a school in Virginia, a more fashionable institution than the one outside Syracuse. Taggart's visit with her proved to be their last meeting. Marie presented him with an ultimatum: either he agreed to turn himself in or they were finished. Confronted, Taggart made his choice. Marie tried to return the engagement ring, but he refused it. "Give it to your family," he said.

As in the past, Taggart had no difficulty finding employment. He worked in the Philadelphia area as a bartender, an auto mechanic, and a construction man with a gang paving a state highway. In this last job, he said, he had so many straw bosses that, deviating from his policy, he admitted his AWOL status to none. While he was on this job, he told me, he forgot his latest cover name, staring uncomprehendingly at a foreman who was yelling, "Hatcher! Hatcher!" Taggart said, "He chewed me out real hard. He should have. When you use a fake name you have to keep telling yourself, 'That's me, that's me, no one else.'" In a different way, Taggart also goofed as a bartender when he allowed himself to disagree about the war with a pair of Martini drinkers. Forming a friendship at the bar, the two had discovered that they both blamed "hippie degenerates" for delaying victory in Indo-China. "I should have moved away from them," Taggart told me. But he didn't, and eventually, as he might have foreseen, the patrons wanted to hear their bartender's opinion. Taggart gave it succinctly: "I'm no hippie, and I think the war stinks." One of the men called Taggart a Communist, and the other summoned the manager, who, hurrying over, told his bartender to beat it, and stood the offended customers another round. There were always lapses waiting to be committed, Taggart continued. Only rarely did he feel practiced in the role of an AWOL, one of those occasions being a spring Sunday that he spent hitchhiking around the Philadelphia countryside. While thumbing rides indiscriminately, he said, he drew a car that contained two state troopers. They asked for his draft card, which he produced forthwith, but Taggart didn't stop there. Gratuitously, he said, he went on extracting one credential after another from his wallet, until the police, bored with his innocence, delivered him to a forest he was curious to explore.

Taggart left Philadelphia in early July, 1970, and he did it, he said, not because of enemies but because of his friends. After a point, he explained, their generosity became a burden. He said, "I couldn't tell anymore what

I'd be able to do if I were on my own. Maybe I'd have felt
that way even if I hadn't been an AWOL." He found it
oppressive, he said, when his hosts inquired solicitously
whether he would like to borrow the family car, or have
his room repainted or, perhaps, recurtained. Taggart said,
"I didn't want four homes, just one—a place of my own."
Gradually, he continued, his attitude toward his benefac-
tors became ambivalent. He admired them for risking
their ordered, comfortable existence in the cause of peace,
but, at the same time, he envied them for what they were
able to risk—families, careers, structured lives. "Without
meaning to, these friends were getting me down," he said.
"They were rubbing it in that I had no future of my own
to speak of. It made me want to leave Philly." The chance
to do so wasn't long in coming. It occurred when a history
professor asked Taggart whether he would be interested
in opening a summer cottage that the professor owned up
in northern New England, near the Canadian border; the
professor and his family planned to go up there in a few
weeks. Taggart took him up, fully aware that he was
accepting yet another favor from yet another thriving
sympathizer. He was too eager, though, for a change of
scene to care. "I was tired of city traffic," Taggart told me.
"I wanted to try again to figure out just where I was
headed. I left for New England feeling the way I had
when I had gone off to Canada."

The history professor's cottage was part of a strange
community, the center of which was a small town whose
economy revolved around a textile factory. The cottage
was six miles from there, amid an expanse of streams and
lakes, farmland, and dense stands of conifers and birches,
all set against the distant backdrop of a hazy mountain
range. But the war was as ever-present as nature, Taggart
told me, for living in neighboring cottages and farm-
houses were scores of AWOLs and draft evaders, a
number of whom maintained themselves in communes;
girl friends were on hand, as were older anti-war activists.
"It was as if the peace movement had gone to the

country," Taggart said. Some people knew the area as
Little Canada, but Taggart rejected the implication that it
had anything to do with Canada. On the contrary, he told
me, he found it heartening that others, like him, chose to
remain on American soil, even though Canada was so
near. Taggart did, however, concede certain resemblances
between American fugitives across the border and those
in the remote spot to which he had just transplanted
himself. Like the deserter colonies in Montreal and
Toronto, he said, the small New England one had its
share of shattered types, such as unemployables and
junkies. As in Canada, too, he went on, there was a small
group of AWOLs interested in guerrilla training, whose
ideology, Taggart said, consisted of a desire to be left
alone. "They slept with shotguns, ready to blow away any
cops," he told me. "They had surprisingly good weapons.
The townspeople had no idea what was going on in their
backwoods." And, as in Canada, Taggart took part in
several guerrilla drills. For himself, he said, he continued
to abjure the use of violence, but more and more he could
see how others might resort to it. "It was the only way to
make things change—that's what some of the guys
believed," he told me. "They'd had enough of waiting for
something to happen."

As far as Taggart's own life went, I gathered, he
occupied himself as resourcefully as he could. Certainly
his first three weeks in New England passed industrious-
ly, the professor's cottage having had a rugged winter;
many windows needed caulking, shingles were missing
from the roof, plumbing problems had come up. When
the professor and his family arrived, they were delighted
with the condition of their house. Predictably, Taggart
told me, the professor offered him a free room. Taggart
declined it. "I wanted to make my break," he said. He
moved into a boarding house in the town, whose citizens
treated him with extraordinary cordiality. He owed this,
he discovered in due course, to his short sideburns and a
couple of sports coats he was fond of wearing. Long

accustomed to the scruffy appearance of the military dropouts living beyond the town limits, the natives hailed Taggart as a model stranger. "I was told I had 'class,'" he recalled. Thanks to the impression he made, Taggart said, he had friends both in the colony and on Main Street—a fact that came out clearly one evening after he had put in a hard afternoon pitching Molotov cocktails with some guerrilla comrades. Waiting for him when he came home, Taggart told me, was the town sheriff, a newly elected official with whom Taggart was on good terms. The sheriff, it appeared, was interested in expanding the force he had inherited; he wanted to know whether Taggart would serve as a deputy. Taggart filled out required forms in triplicate, but, as luck would have it, the town's selectmen didn't vote the necessary funds. "That was too bad," Taggart said. "It would have made a good headline—'Deputy Sheriff Arrested as AWOL.'"

During the summer months, Taggart worked for a builder, who had all the contracts he could handle, mostly for homes. As a result, Taggart said, he became an adept plumber, passing a state test that earned him a plumber's license. In the fall, he found employment at the textile factory, operating machines on its assembly line. Despite his unexpected popularity, Taggart told me, he kept to himself. He read more than he ever had before. He was no intellectual, he said, but at this particular period he seemed drawn to books on philosophy. "Maybe being in the country had something to do with that," he suggested. On one occasion, he said, he stayed up late composing a long letter to the President in which he recounted his grievances in detail. "I threw it away," Taggart said. "Guys like me were a dime a dozen around the country. The President must have had bushels of letters like mine." Many nights, he said, he lay awake ruminating on how his future could come out nice and neat. In the stillness of the boarding house, which sat at the edge of a thin woods, it began to cross his mind with some regularity that he would have to give himself up. He fought off the thought, deliberately rekindling his anger against the government. He was jolted, he said, that he should be thinking along lines of surrender, but the thought had likely been germinating a long time. A thousand things, he conjectured, could have led up to it. Only recently, he said, he had been upset by a small, foolish incident. Roofing a cottage one afternoon, he had gazed at a landscape of open fields and had prosaically played with the notion that it was probably a good time for someone to invest in local real estate. In the next instant, Taggart said, it had hit him that the investor couldn't possibly be himself, for as an AWOL he couldn't invest in real estate or anything else. He told me, "The way I saw it, each contract I signed with a fake name might be something else that could get me into trouble. Planning was out. It made me feel old, knowing that."

Taggart came out of his shell, he said, about the time he went to work at the textile factory. It was autumn then, and some—but not most—of the AWOLs had moved on, gypsylike, to warmer parts of the country. Among the members of the colony who remained was a girl, Ann Wood, with whom he formed a relationship. It had none of the ups and downs he had known with Marie, he said, for Ann was of an undemanding, encouraging nature. She was also more political-minded than Marie, he told me, involving him in a project to drive over the border and bring back two close friends of hers—an AWOL and his girl, who were broke in Montreal. Taggart found the pair jobs at the textile factory; they were still in New England, he told me, and had built themselves a small house there. "They write me. They're watching my case," he said. Once he met Ann, Taggart said, his spirits rose. "I felt ready to try again to make it as an AWOL," he said. "I didn't know whether that could be done anywhere, but certainly the town wasn't the place. It offered no choices." He wouldn't consider Philadelphia, he said, but Syracuse was the right size. He had friends there; it had enough political activity to satisfy Ann; he was certain the police there had lost interest in him by then. In February, 1971, in a driving snowstorm, he and Ann took a bus for upstate New York.

Syracuse was Taggart's last stop; he left it, in handcuffs, early in 1972. Looking back, Taggart said, he found it hard to believe that he was there a whole year. "The time flew," he told me. "I always felt busy, stewing over whether to come in or to go on trying to make it." Outwardly, though, the year unfolded smoothly. He and Ann, he said, rented a small, bright apartment in a building tenanted largely by students attending Syracuse University nearby; Taggart audited a philosophy course there. Thanks to his plumber's license, he said, he was soon earning a hundred and fifteen dollars a week mending drains and pumps. Ann liked his Syracuse friends, all of whom, Taggart observed, seemed to take his reappearance for granted. "Maybe AWOLs drifted in and out of their lives all the time," he said. It was while he was introducing Ann around, he recalled, that they accepted an invitation to a party at a friend's house. As they arrived, Taggart spotted a familiar car parked directly in front of the house. The car belonged to Dorn, the snowmobile salesman, who had called the police more than a year ago. "We went in," Taggart told me. "With Ann along, I was sure I'd keep my cool." Dozens of guests were in an outsize living room, drinking, turning on, buzzing with talk. He was glad that it was a big party, Taggart said; it made it easy to see Dorn alone, so to speak. "I didn't know what I'd say," Taggart told me. Everything was over fast. As he and Ann advanced into the room, he found Dorn literally at his feet. He was sitting cross-legged against a wall talking to a girl. When he saw Taggart, he rose slowly, his eyes searching for an exit. "I'd forgot how tall he was," Taggart said. "He started to leave, and I grabbed him. 'I'm not going to hit you,' I told him. 'You're all messed up—you, with your

boozing and ratting on me. But you haven't hurt me. I've
travelled, I've studied, I've met brilliant people, I'm
making it.' Ann hooked her arm in mine and pulled me
across the room. She knew I wasn't talking to Dorn but
just going on about myself."

Plumbing began to pall for Taggart after six months.
He preferred being around cars, he said, and, scouting for
something in that field, he found a job selling new cars
and occasionally repairing them. "It was the best job I'd
ever had," Taggart told me. His employer made it even
more than that. A man in his early fifties, a former
well-known athlete, and a regular churchgoer, the owner
of the auto agency, Michael Bass, was deeply impressed
when Taggart, in keeping with his policy, revealed that
he was an AWOL. Taggart told me, "It seemed to get to
him that he had my trust. Mr. Bass stood up at his desk
and paced around his office, then sat down again and said,
'I'm not saying for you to do it, but if you give yourself up
I want you to know that your job will be waiting for you
after you come out.' He asked me all sorts of questions
about myself. He asked to meet Ann. It was all a personal
thing with him, what he was doing. Politically, Mr. Bass
was probably on the conservative side—his agency had
been doing all right for a long time. I couldn't figure out
what was going on, except that maybe he thought he
ought to stick his neck out on something before he got too
old."

Whatever Mr. Bass's reason was, Taggart recognized
his offer as a break. It wasn't without its pressures,
however, he said, for, out of the blue, his employer's offer
guaranteed Taggart the future that he had resolved he
must have before he would surrender. "It was up to me
now to put up or shut up," Taggart told me. Confronted
by his own bargain, he said, he cast about for ways of
circumventing it, but nothing that came to his mind, no
matter how freely he let it wander, could do away with
the need for him to give himself up. All that his casting
about did, Taggart told me, was cause him to review once

more the kind of life he was leading. "It wasn't good," he said. He despised his unending reliance on subterfuge. It shamed him, he said, to take people into his confidence only when it suited some design. Mr. Bass's generous response had left him feeling that way, he said. Naturally, he continued, he talked things over with Ann, but he found that, unintentionally, she said the wrong thing. Like Mr. Bass, she said she would stick by him, whatever his decision, and that, Taggart told me, merely exerted further pressure. "I started giving cops the widest possible berth," he said. "If I saw one a block away, I'd cross the street to get out of his path. It wouldn't be right to be caught now. I knew I was about to make up my mind, and I wanted the freedom to do so. Ann called it my last luxury."

Taggart nearly lost that luxury a month after his talk with Mr. Bass, when an altercation took place between two fellow-tenants of the apartment house, both students. He and Ann, alone in their apartment one midnight, were startled by a frantic knocking at their door. When he opened it, a bespectacled, bookish-looking student brushed past him, seeking safety in the apartment. Before Taggart could shut the door, the second student, an upstate Indian, brandishing a length of metal pipe, was also inside the apartment. As Taggart planted himself between the two, the frightened student related that the Indian, whose apartment was next to his own, had been playing records extremely loud and that he had asked him to lower the volume; for some reason, the Indian had taken offense, and here they were. The Indian now tried again to move on his bookish neighbor, and Taggart told him to drop the pipe. For an answer, the upstater swung it at Taggart, who, barely dodging it, wrested it from his attacker. In a matter of minutes, the night visitors were gone, and Taggart, in possession of the pipe, thought the incident closed. He was mistaken. Half an hour later, someone new was at the door—a policeman, asking to enter. Taggart immediately ordered Ann to leave by a

back door. "When AWOLs are picked up, their girls are
often also taken in," he said. But the cop hadn't come on
AWOL business. He was accompanied by the Indian,
who, seeing the pipe on the floor, triumphantly exclaimed, "There it is!" The officer nodded soberly and
said he was arresting Taggart for having assaulted the
Indian. "I didn't ask the cop whether he had a warrant,"
Taggart told me. "As an AWOL, I didn't dare antagonize
him. Actually, I didn't think about a warrant at the time.
Everything that was happening was too crazy." In the
station house, the cop, continuing to practice his own
brand of due process, took Taggart's fingerprints, and
that, as Taggart put it, had him sweating; checked out by
the F.B.I.'s computer in Washington, he said, the
fingerprints could be used to expose him as an AWOL. As
Taggart pondered this, the policeman, hunched over a
blank form, began a routine interview. It came to an
abrupt halt when he discovered that Taggart wasn't a
student. Judging by his annoyed expression, Taggart said,
the cop had assumed otherwise. Skeptically, he challenged Taggart for his employer's name, which the officer
recognized. It was two in the morning, but he rang Mr.
Bass, who vouched for his employee. "He says you're
O.K.," the policeman told Taggart. "Now beat it, and let's
have no sass."

Taggart walked home—a distance of ten or twelve
blocks. He told me he was glad to be by himself on the
dark, deserted streets. Their quiet, he said, helped him
reach a decision that only he could make. "There was no
delaying it, not after the close call I'd had," Taggart told
me. Emerging from the police station, he said, he realized
acutely that everything in his AWOL's world was subject
to instant disappearance. Taggart said, "While I was
being fingerprinted, I could see my landlord carting off
the furniture I'd bought. I could see the cops towing away
my car, and my never being able to get it back." His
friends, too, Taggart went on, could have disappeared,
among them Mr. Bass and, of course, Ann, who, as he

presently found out, was anxiously waiting for him in the apartment. Walking home that night, he said, he saw with hopeless clarity that the whole idea of making it was nothing more than a mirage. Speaking in a faltering voice—the one time he did so, at any of our various meetings—Taggart said, "The achievements that can make someone else feel good won't do the same for an AWOL. He knows that the more he has the more he stands to lose, suddenly, without claim, no matter how meaningless it may be to others."

In the morning, at the automobile agency, Taggart informed Mr. Bass that he was giving himself up. That afternoon, he told me, the two of them visited Mr. Bass's lawyer, who advised the AWOL to volunteer no information to the authorities after he surrendered. The advice, it developed, wasn't easy to heed, for when Taggart, together with Mr. Bass, reported to a precinct house the following day, the police eyed him as an impostor. "I had to talk my way in," Taggart said. "I volunteered every detail I could think of to prove when and where I had been in what unit. It broke Mr. Bass up." The police were forty-five minutes confirming Taggart's facts. When they had done so, Mr. Bass shook Taggart's hand warmly and took his leave. With his departure, the police gave Taggart their undivided attention. "They put me in leg irons as well as handcuffs. I spent the night in jail," Taggart said.

Shortly after Taggart rose the next morning, he told me, a member of the Shore Patrol, carrying a nightstick, was on hand to deliver him to the brig at the United States Naval Station, in Brooklyn. Now only in handcuffs, Taggart left the precinct house for the Syracuse airport. Once the plane was aloft, his hands were freed, in accordance with a regulation aimed at helping passengers in the event of accident. Taggart's unencumbered state, he said, seemed to unnerve his escort. "He wouldn't let me have coffee; he said I might throw it in his face," Taggart told me. He had no such intention, he assured me, but he was in a sullen mood the entire flight. He had imagined he would experience a deep sense of relief on giving himself up, he said, but that wasn't turning out to be the case. On the contrary, it rankled him that he should have had to negotiate his peace through genuflection. He resented the government's power, he said, asserting that there wasn't a shred of virtue to be detected in its war. He also felt an impatience to know his brother's opinions, he said; he wanted them to compare their tours of duty. The two Taggarts, I was told, hadn't communicated in years, but Taggart had learned through a friend from home he had run into that his brother had been to Vietnam as a Green Beret and had been honorably discharged with all sorts of ribbons. Unlike himself, Taggart told me, his brother had had reservations about the war before enlisting. He had joined the Berets, Taggart said, only because he foresaw a day when a son of his might ask, "Daddy, what did you do in the war?" On the plane, he had turned the question on himself. He told me, "The best I could say to any son of mine would be 'I didn't kill anyone.' I certainly wouldn't claim I'd been any kind of hero, and I don't think my brother can do that, either, for what he did. For Americans, I think, it's been pretty much a war without heroes."

Ten minutes before the plane landed, Taggart's guard fell asleep, the handcuffs dangling from a pocket. Taggart thought of discarding them, but didn't pursue the idea for long. He was too busy contemplating his immediate future. He didn't relish the likelihood of a second stay in the brig, he said. When the plane finally touched down at Kennedy, he shook his captor awake and eagerly extended his wrists. "I wanted to get whatever I had coming to me over and done with," he said.

Once Taggart arrived in Brooklyn, where he awaited his court-martial, he phoned his parents to say he was all right, and they offered him their savings for his defense. His brother phoned and said, "I'd take your route, Harry, if I had it to do over again." The call, Taggart said, didn't make him feel right or wrong, only conscious of a deep

bond with his contemporaries. He had no idea when he
would stand trial; the court calendar, he had been
informed, was heavy. Two months after being flown to
the Naval Station, he was given a weekend pass, which he
used for a visit to Ann and Mr. Bass. They restated their
promises of support, come what may, which gratified
Taggart, who told me, "All the way to Syracuse, by bus, I
thought that maybe they wouldn't say that. A long time
ago, I trusted anyone." For the moment, he said, he was
pleased that he wasn't in the brig. He had been, his first
two days in Brooklyn, but, fortunately, he said, a
lieutenant had reasoned that Taggart wasn't likely to bolt
after having surrendered on his own. As a result, Taggart
said, he had been carrying out a variety of chores, among
them chauffeuring admirals, helping construct a Navy
Exchange, and driving a truck. He had also pulled
military-police duty, in which capacity, his nightstick at
the ready, he stood watch while men in trouble, like
himself, made emergency calls home. Every now and
then, on hanging up, one of his charges was apt to mutter,
"I've got to get out of this place." Taggart never
responded. "What could I tell him?" he said. "We were in
the same boat."

6

LOVE OF COUNTRY

🚩 🚩 🚩 🚩 🚩

Susan Cook Russo, a slight, reticent brunette with straight hair and luminous black eyes, was twenty-one when she came East to fill her first teaching job. Just graduated from Michigan State, *magna cum laude*, she was eager to embark on a career of teaching art to high-school students. The time was late August of 1969 and the place Rochester, New York, for which Mrs. Russo and her husband, John, who was also a teacher, had chosen to leave the Midwest. The two, who had been married only a few months, were from East Lansing, Michigan, where they had been classmates in high school and college. John Russo, a short, mild-mannered man with a brown beard, had a job awaiting him in the science department of a public high school in Rochester. The post that Mrs. Russo had found was at the James E. Sperry High School, in Henrietta, a fast-growing middle-class suburb five miles from Rochester. The principal there, Donald A. Loughlin, had seen Mrs. Russo in May, shortly before her commencement, and had given

her a careful hearing. It had gone well. Mrs. Russo had
formidable credentials to offer, among them her outstanding academic record and glowing letters of reference; the
aspirant art teacher could also claim a mother who was a
professor of art education; besides these assets, Mrs.
Russo had worked her way through college, as a waitress,
a tutor, and a librarian, and she had won several
scholarships. Recalling the interview nearly four years
later, in 1973, when I talked with him, Loughlin told me,
"She made an excellent impression." He said it with stern
reluctance, for by the spring of 1970, after Mrs. Russo had
been on his staff for eight months, Loughlin and she
wished that they had never met. By then, like other
Americans, they had discovered that they had irreconcila-
ble conceptions of patriotism, the principal being
adamant that the school pay daily homage to the
American flag, the new teacher rejecting the Pledge of
Allegiance as a sham, her opposition based on her country's
war in Indo-China and on widespread poverty at home.

By the spring of 1970, too, the differences between the
principal and the new instructor were hardly a private
quarrel. Loughlin's superior, Superintendent of Schools
Richard E. Ten Haken, had entered the conflict, as had
the district board of education, both siding with
Loughlin. The press covered the controversy. Students
were involved. The community's taxpayers spoke up,
preponderantly in favor of the school principal. By the
time Mrs. Russo's first year as a teacher was at an end, she
had been fired, summarily informed by Ten Haken that
her probationary period of three years—a requirement for
beginning teachers—had been cancelled. Mrs. Russo's
reaction was swift. She sued Sperry's hierarchy for
reinstatement and fifty thousand dollars in damages. The
litigation has now been through the courts. The first legal
ruling went against Mrs. Russo, but she won on appeal.
That ruling didn't leave her feeling victorious, though,
for in the years since her falling out with the Sperry
principal her teaching career remained at a halt, her
future an impenetrable fog. John Russo told me, "We

came East for new experiences, but not for the one that has befallen Susan. It's getting to be like a nightmare from which there's no waking up."

Curious about the reasons for Mrs. Russo's undoing, I flew to Rochester to talk with her and her husband as well as with those who had joined in having her cashiered. Naturally, while in Rochester, I inquired about Mrs. Russo's suit, but it was her show of defiance that drew me to the city. What, I had wondered on first hearing about the case, could have prompted Mrs. Russo to heed her unprofitable impulse? How could she, a rookie teacher, and an outlander at that, dare to disturb the order of things in a suburban paradise? I wondered, too, what sort of life she had been leading since her dismissal, and whether her outlook on saluting the flag had changed. Did she regret what she had done? The Russos freely answered these and other questions, discussing them with me in their home, a modest frame house they had rented two years before. We talked in the living room, a small, dimly lit oblong that was furnished with dilapidated easy chairs, their aging process no doubt speeded by the family pet, a restless Irish setter. Mrs. Russo's work decorated the room—drawings, prints, and, prominently, a sculpture made of stuffed, bizarrely shaped pieces of fabric treated with a metallic sheen. A straightforward, earnest girl in jeans, Mrs. Russo had large, searching eyes—her most striking feature. Glancing at her husband, who was sitting across the room, Mrs. Russo said that he was on hand at her urging; she was unaccustomed to being interviewed, she explained, and counted on his presence to lend her fortitude. Having said this, Mrs. Russo proceeded—quite calmly, I thought—to give me an account of her difficulties. As she had testified in court, they had begun the first minute of the first day she met with students, early in September, 1969. "But I didn't know it, and neither did anyone else," she said. That morning—and on each succeeding one, as Mrs. Russo was to discover—the Sperry day opened with a broadcast of the Pledge of Allegiance. Piped throughout the school over a public-address system, the Pledge reached Mrs. Russo's ears, as it did everyone else's, in the form of a male voice, anonymous and somewhat fumbling. With an experienced teacher, Mrs. Kathryn Adams, Mrs. Russo was then overseeing two dozen tenth-grade students who were checking in for the day at their homeroom. On hearing the Pledge, she told me, the students rose from their chairs and, facing an American flag at the front of the room, placed their hands over their hearts with a practiced motion. Mrs. Adams also rose to her feet. Mrs. Russo followed suit. Directly behind her, she could hear her colleague, like the students, reciting in unison with the disembodied voice. Mrs. Russo herself remained silent; as she subsequently testified, there had been no such ceremony at the schools she had attended in East Lansing. "Everything was over in seconds," Mrs. Russo said. The Pledge's single sentence rendered, the students turned away from the flag and, resuming their preparations for the day, listened to a flood of announcements, also piped in, that dealt with a variety of extracurricular activities—committee meetings, football practice, tickets for a rock concert. All told, Mrs. Russo estimated, the homeroom meeting took perhaps ten minutes, after which the students went off to their regular classes. Mrs. Russo told me, "When I got home that afternoon, I asked John whether the public school he was teaching at also gave the Pledge. He said no, and we talked about other things."

The following morning, and for months of mornings thereafter, the scene repeated itself: the class pledged allegiance while Mrs. Russo stood mute. No one seemed to make anything of her seconds of silence. She herself had her mind on the hours of her working day. Sperry made her glad she had become a teacher. Each day, she said, she felt increasingly at home in her profession. Faculty colleagues proved congenial. Modern and bright, the Sperry building had excellent facilities for her art students. It was gratifying to win their attention and to awaken their interest in art. Her absorption in her duties never waned. Often, she said, she remained behind after school hours, her classroom a redoubt for artistically inclined students, only slightly their teacher's junior. One of Mrs. Russo's students presently won a national award—the first in the district's history—and this was a feat for which the novice instructor was publicly saluted, as Dr. Ten Haken later acknowledged in court. Mrs. Russo's morale was afforded a further boost when, on April 17, 1970, one of Loughlin's assistants, after visiting her classroom on several occasions, filed a teacher-observation report that was practically perfect, the assistant principal finding no fault with her in such disparate categories as planning and organization, classroom leadership, and teaching techniques. The report, which was introduced as an exhibit at the trial, states, "Mrs. Russo has a congenial, relaxed personality and meets students at their level. . . . [Her] teaching methods and techniques appear to be resourceful and appropriate to individualized instruction in a creative atmosphere. . . . The teacher plans basic time periods for each project but is flexible in regard to completion time so as to allow for individual differences. . . . Student participation has generally appeared to be at a high level—most seem busily at work generally."

Three days after the assistant principal entered his report, the morning in Mrs. Russo's homeroom at last began differently: Loughlin arrived to watch the recitation of the Pledge. Framed in the doorway, the principal fixed his eyes on Mrs. Russo as she faced the flag, and, again, as had been occurring since September, her lips remained unmoving, her hands at her sides. Loughlin was present, he later testified, because, indirectly, he had learned from another teacher that Mrs. Russo was not participating in the flag ritual. Mrs. Russo doubted whether the teacher, whose identity she knew, meant her any harm. "We were friends," she said. "She was chatting idly about me with another teacher, and soon her words reached Don Loughlin." Mrs. Russo said that after Loughlin appeared at the homeroom her confrontation with him wasn't long in coming. The next morning, before homeroom, she was in his office, summoned there for what proved to be the first of several encounters, each increasingly chilly. Their substance may be found in the court record. Asked what Loughlin said at their first meeting, Mrs. Russo testified, "To the best of my recollection, he asked me specifically why I didn't say the Pledge in the classroom. I responded that I didn't agree with the wording of the Pledge, and it was a matter of my own personal conscience, and I couldn't be hypocritical about what I believed in. He asked me whether I considered that I would be an example to students whether I said it or not, and I replied . . . that I felt I was a better example by being truthful to my beliefs than by saying something that I didn't believe in. He never asked me to say the Pledge, but he did ask me to think about what he had said." Earlier in her testimony, Mrs. Russo had said, "I believe in America, and I am generally proud to be an American, but I object to saying the Pledge for basically two reasons. First of all, I don't think that anyone can demand the recitation of an oath of allegiance. I think loyalty is better proved through daily actions and the way you behave as an American citizen, but, more importantly, I object to the actual wording of the Pledge, because the words 'liberty and justice for all' are inaccurate, and I feel we are hypocritical in saying that as a truth." Recalling his meeting with Mrs. Russo, Loughlin testified, "I . . . asked Mrs. Russo why she wasn't saluting the flag, and she indicated that she had not been saluting the flag since the beginning of the year, and I asked for her reasons, and she said [because of] the part 'with liberty and justice for all,' and I think we discussed some of the social ills and so forth that she was concerned about. . . . I . . . explained that 'liberty and justice for all' were ideals that we were striving for."

On May 1st, Loughlin paid a second visit to Mrs.

Russo's homeroom, and he had her report to his office that same afternoon. In court, the following year, a defense attorney asked him how that meeting had come about, and he answered, "I asked to meet with Mrs. Russo after again observing her . . . not saluting the flag." The testimony continued:

> Q.: What was the conversation between you and her at that time?
> A.: I told Mrs. Russo that I was not going to recommend her for reappointment. She asked the reason, and I said I did not have to give a reason.
> Q.: Did you discuss with her during that conversation the alternatives of resignation versus termination?
> A.: I told her that I thought it would be in the best interest of all concerned if she would resign.

On May 4th, Mrs. Russo wrote Loughlin, "I will not resign, as I feel there is no justification for my leaving. I believe that I have more than adequately demonstrated my desire and ability to teach children through my actions this past year. If the reason for my contract not being renewed is politically oriented, I cannot with just conscience accept this decision." A week later, Loughlin sent Ten Haken a message saying, "I recommend that Mrs. Russo's probationary appointment not be renewed for the 1970–71 school year and that her responsibilities be terminated effective June 30."

Word of Mrs. Russo's homeroom conduct could not have reached Loughlin at a more inopportune moment. In the past few months, it appeared, the Pledge of Allegiance had become a thorny, time-consuming issue for the principal, who, incidentally, had yet to complete his own probationary period. In the academic year before Mrs. Russo's arrival, a taped Pledge had been piped over Sperry's public-address system, but a complaint had been lodged that this made the saluting ceremony "mechanical"; as a result, Loughlin had arranged for the Pledge to be given live, its broadcaster usually an assistant principal. Toward the end of 1969, court decisions in New York City and elsewhere made it a question whether students anywhere need pledge allegiance to the flag. And at Sperry, with the coming of spring, a handful of activists—twenty-five of them, perhaps—bestirred themselves to the extent of letting the school board know that they had heard of these court decisions. Seeking to appease the small group, which included the president of the student council, the board passed a resolution that extolled the morning ritual but provided that students could stay seated and silent during the Pledge "on religious grounds or because of conscientious objections." The resolution threw Henrietta into an uproar, its passage denounced as a sop to unpatriotic elements. Sperry was deluged with protests. Editorials appeared in local papers. Rochester organizations expressed shock. Parents phoned and wrote school-board members. A petition was presented, signed by three hundred and fifty residents, who declared, "You don't stand for the Flag!!! We won't stand for the budget!!!" The local teachers' union, to which Mrs. Russo belonged, called the school board's action "intolerable and certainly not in the best interests of the school, community, and our country."

It was when the storm over the resolution was barely under way that Loughlin heard of his art teacher's deportment. "That was all he needed; Susan never had a chance," John Russo said. In his opinion, she offered a ready target for the community's wrath—a solitary, conquerable figure who loomed as a threat to the general stability. Speaking as dispassionately as she could, Mrs. Russo told me that she could almost understand her predicament. To her way of thinking, it was related to the fact that the town's taxpayers—professional men, highly skilled mechanics, Eastman Kodak officials—had worked hard for the comforts of their life in Henrietta; if their children could remain seated in the presence of the flag, she theorized, it would be as though they were repudiating the fruits of their parents' labor. In any event,

Mrs. Russo went on, the townspeople came out in large numbers on April 28th to attend a school-board meeting held in the Sperry cafeteria. Describing the scene, Ten Haken testified, "That was a packed meeting. All of the seats were taken. We had people standing in the back and around the sides and even into the hall, and many people spoke concerning the . . . resolution that the board adopted concerning the flag." The clerk's minutes record that about twenty-five members of the audience rose to inveigh against the resolution; as the audience applauded, one parent, a father, advanced to the front of the cafeteria and, pointing a finger at each of the school-board respresentatives, warned them that they would be turned out of office if the resolution wasn't repealed; the matter, it was finally decided, would be put to a vote at the board's next meeting, on May 12th.

By then, however, the situation was exacerbated, for world events had intruded themselves into Henrietta's crisis: America had invaded Cambodia, and four protesting students had been killed at Kent State University. When the president of Sperry's student council and a few other activists saw fit to identify Mrs. Russo's plight with the nation's Cambodian venture, it just about sealed her fate. In court, a defense attorney asked Loughlin, "Is it fair to say that during this particular period . . . there was some unrest or feeling of protest among the student body?" Loughlin said yes, and the testimony continued:

> Q.: What did you observe, see, or hear on this general subject of protest?
> A.: Well, there were students that were refusing to salute the flag, and that was handled by the administrators and the assistant principals. Also, on May 7th, we had a student attempt to take over the student-council-election assembly.
> Q.: What took place on that occasion?
> A.: . . . We had between fifteen and sixteen hundred youngsters in the gymnasium. At that time the student-council president, Charles Petrin, decided that he was going to talk to the students about Kent State and Cambodia.

Loughlin had ordered the student leader to stick to the
agenda at hand but had agreed to let him address students
during each of the four lunch periods at Sperry.

> Q.: And was the subject of Mrs. Russo discussed . . .?
> A.: Yes.

In cross-examining Mrs. Russo, the defense attorney
probed to see whether she had incited students to come to
her aid. Denying this, she testified that she had had
nothing to do with a petition circulated in her behalf. She
did admit having been in the auditorium during one of
the early lunch periods when the student-council
president gave a speech, the point of which was that her
impending dismissal was in key with the "repression"
that the United States government was visiting on Cambodia. Asked what she had done on hearing the speech,
Mrs. Russo said, "I asked him to stop it."

There was little suspense about the May 12th meeting.
It wasn't even well attended, so foregone was its outcome.
The new resolution was indeed passed, as well as a set of
accompanying "administrative regulations" stipulating
that faculty members were to "exert appropriate professional leadership" in getting pupils to stand during the
Pledge ceremony, and that refractory students faced
suspension "for insubordination or disorderly conduct."
Only eight or ten students were in the audience, and their
opposition was ineffectual, as was that of a few adult
opponents. The minutes of the meeting show that John
Russo was present and asked a question. He inquired
"what the board's position would be if a teacher does not
believe that America stands for liberty and justice for all,
and therefore did not participate in the Pledge of
Allegiance to the flag." In reply, he was told that "this
would be a regrettable situation" and that it "would be
faced if and when it happens."

Two days after the meeting, Loughlin issued a
two-page memorandum containing what he described as

"a suggested line of reasoning which might be profitably pursued by the homeroom teacher in counselling with a student who chooses not to stand and participate in the daily Pledge of Allegiance." In it, the principal cautioned his teachers against resorting to "sarcasm and derogatory remarks" in coping with students who choked on the Pledge's last phrase—"with liberty and justice for all." He noted, "A more appropriate tack might be to emphasize that these ideals are just that—ideals to which America aspires. They have always been a sort of beacon guiding the direction in which America has moved, albeit not always in a straight line or at top speed. . . . The only way that we can bring America up to [these] ideals . . . is to work through the existing machinery for change, and not to offend large numbers of people. Even the most vocal anti-war groups have recently come around to accepting this as a fact of life. . . . The teacher might, therefore, indicate to the student that to remain seated during the Pledge . . . creates greater antagonism in the minds of those who have the power to make changes."

Mrs. Russo didn't wait for the axe to fall. That was due to happen on June 23rd, at the school board's final meeting of the year. Between May 12th and that date, she instituted her legal action. "I was tired of being on the receiving end," Mrs. Russo told me. As a result of inquiries she made at her union local, she and her husband found their way to Albany and the offices of Richard R. Rowley, counsel of the New York State Teachers Association. Much depended on the visit, as the Russos were aware, for not only could Rowley choose to represent Mrs. Russo but he could also recommend to the association that it underwrite the legal costs of her suit. The visit proved successful. Rowley told me later that as he heard her out he was strongly drawn to her case, because she intended to plead it solely on grounds of conscience; most flag-saluting litigants, he said, invoked religious scruples. Mrs. Russo had no pretenses on that score; nor, for that matter, she volunteered to the attorney, did her parents, both of them fitful Episcopalians. Before making up his mind, Rowley asked her all manner of questions, including a particular series that elicited negative answers: Was Mrs. Russo having an affair with anyone at Sperry? How about John Russo at his school? Were she and her husband into drugs? Alcohol? Was the Russo marriage on the rocks?

For the Russos, the board's June 23rd meeting unfolded in an atmosphere of tension. They had come to the school cafeteria, where the meeting was held, hoping that Mrs. Russo's situation would be publicly aired. But the case wasn't on the evening's agenda. At eleven-fifteen or so, the board, with Ten Haken, retired to Loughlin's conference room to hold closed deliberations; the audience—about fifty people—was apprised that it could pass on the board's decisions when the board returned to the cafeteria to resume its public session. John Russo told me that the sight of the departing board was one that had stayed in his memory. He said, "Watching each member file out, I knew for sure there wasn't a thing I could do for Susan. I think I learned to hate." In its executive session, the court record shows, the board gave most of its time to a discussion of Mrs. Russo, the upshot of which was the drafting of a resolution that the "probationary appointment of Susan C. Russo be and it hereby is terminated, effective upon the expiration of 30 days after service upon said Susan C. Russo of the notice of termination as required by Section 3019-a of the Education Law. . . ." When the board finally came back to the cafeteria, one of its members moved that the resolution be adopted, and a colleague seconded the motion forthwith. During the trial, Rowley asked the seconder, "The motion was all written out, wasn't it?," to which the witness replied, "No, I don't think so. It wasn't that hard to do." The motion carried unanimously. The board reconvened in public session for only five minutes. But there wasn't any public. It was one-twenty-five in the morning, and no one had waited around for the board to reappear; even the Russos had left.

Mrs. Russo kept going, as she put it. She didn't dare do otherwise, she told me, for inaction might invite a corrosive bitterness, for which she felt there was no basis, since it wasn't as though all were lost. As she pointed out, she had found Rowley and had filed her suit, and could now look forward to her trial. When Rowley warned her that the trial might be quite a while in coming, Mrs. Russo enrolled at the Rochester Institute of Technology to study for a Master of Fine Arts degree. She had planned to try for it some years later, she said, when she and John would have the savings to see her through the two years it ordinarily took to earn the degree. Enrolling prematurely, Mrs. Russo said, involved borrowing from banks. "John and I were broke most of the time," she told me. During her first year at the Institute, she worked as a library clerk, and the following year she was the only one in her field of twenty to be awarded a graduate assistantship. Between her jobs and her courses, Mrs. Russo said, she was busy seven days a week—almost enough to keep her from thinking about Sperry. She was in the school studio, working, every chance she got. She said, "The more I sculpted the more I found I liked being alone. It was something new for me. I've always been a private person, but I felt especially so after the business at Sperry."

Mrs. Russo's case was heard in the United States District Court for the Western District of New York, Judge Harold P. Burke presiding, on July 7, 1971—more than a year after the climactic meeting in the Sperry cafeteria. The trial lasted two days. Smiling reminiscently, Mrs. Russo said she had entered the courtroom confident of a happy ending; right was on her side, she had believed, and it would surely rout her adversaries, bringing about her vindication and her return to Sperry. Apart from teaching her that law and justice weren't necessarily the same thing, the trial proved an unedifying experience. It did, however, afford Mrs. Russo an occasion for ruminating on the nature of the flag, and that was surprising, she said, since the trial touched relatively little on the flag. Brushing aside Rowley's contention that Mrs. Russo had acted within her constitutional rights while she was at Sperry, defense lawyers sought to minimize her refusal to recite the Pledge as the cause of her dismissal. Characterizing it as "insubordination" rather than a lack of patriotism, the defense lumped it with other alleged manifestations of disobedience.

One of them, it was argued, was a refusal to teach ceramics; interrogation by her own lawyer brought out the fact that Mrs. Russo, speaking hypothetically, had remarked that if she were ever called upon to teach ceramics she wouldn't do it, because she considered herself unqualified; the remark had emerged from a protest made to Loughlin by Mrs. Russo and two other art teachers—Sperry's entire art department—that a ceramics teacher Loughlin had just appointed wasn't qualified for the post. Another of Mrs. Russo's shortcomings, it was asserted, was that she had once missed hall duty—an assignment whose purpose was to hurry tardy students to their homerooms; under cross-examination, Mrs. Russo stated that other teachers had missed hall duty, owing to vague instructions. Mrs. Russo was also accused of an "uncooperative attitude" toward performing extracurricular activities, and Rowley responded by pointing out his client's after-school services, among them extensive art coaching, the planning of student exhibits, and work as sophomore-class adviser.

The defense made much of the fact that Rowley had become Mrs. Russo's lawyer before she was actually fired. Dwelling on the point, the Sperry lawyers cited it as clear evidence that the New York State Teachers Association had fastened on Mrs. Russo's case as a means of bringing about "instant tenure"—that is, doing away with the requirement that teachers serve out a probationary period of three years before acquiring tenure. On the basis of provisions of New York State's Education Law, the defense insisted that probationers weren't entitled to explanations of why they failed their tryouts. Arguing this, the defense said, "[It] is the duty of the superintendent of schools and of the board of education to evaluate teachers as to their fitness to be appointed as teachers on permanent tenure. . . . The paramount public interest requires that the superintendent and the members of the board of education shall be able to carry out their duties and obligations, under the statute, without fear of being subjected to claims for damage. . . ." Defense witnesses were often hazy about Mrs. Russo's reputed derelictions, other than her failure to recite the Pledge. One such witness, after admitting that he was having trouble recalling specific acts of insubordination on Mrs. Russo's part, quickly regained his memory when Rowley inquired, "But you do remember about the flag salute?"

"Certainly, sure," the witness replied.

The longer Mrs. Russo sat in the courtroom, she told me, the more remote she felt from her own trial; the more the proceedings bypassed the heart of her suit, as she had conceived of it, the more they appeared to diminish the flag. In contemplating the trial, Mrs. Russo said, she had imagined that it would turn on beliefs and ideals and other matters of breadth that the flag conjured up for her. It was deflating, she said, to listen to the haggling over "instant tenure" (which, she testified, she hadn't previously heard of). As a "flag-saluting case," in the jargon of lawyers, Mrs. Russo felt herself the creature of impersonal forces engaged in a power struggle. Fixing her black eyes on me, she said, "The flag is power." She spoke in a measured tone, as though making known a well-earned insight. In the past, Mrs. Russo went on, she hadn't thought of the flag as an emblem of self-interest, but once this did occur to her, it seemed to give her a grasp of everything that was going on in the courtroom. She then even saw her own lawyer in a new light, for increasing his own power, she conjectured, might well have been one of his motives in deciding to take her on as a client. She could understand now the caution he had displayed in coming to that decision: his influence as counsel for the New York State Teachers Association stood to be impaired or enhanced, depending on how she fared. As for the defendants, Mrs. Russo said, their stake was plain: they wanted interference from no one in ruling their roost. She envied them the aplomb with which they accepted their power. Loughlin, for instance, in discussing Mrs. Russo's dismissal, had had no hesitation in testifying, "I did not have to give a reason." And Ten Haken had been the soul of poise. A handsome, imposing man, Mrs. Russo said, he had approached her plaintiff's chair and solicitously inquired of her how things were going; he had also come to court with his two young daughters and two nieces, all dressed in white. ("I thought it would be an educational experience for them," Ten Haken told me at his home.) But far more impressive to Mrs. Russo than her adversaries' aplomb, she said, was the conviction with which they testified. She found that disconcerting. As she watched each of them leave the stand, she said, the confusing thought gradually took hold that neither she nor they necessarily represented right or wrong. "It was simply that we had different ways of being patriotic," she told me. Naturally, Mrs. Russo preferred her own outlook. She believed that criticism could strengthen the country, keeping it lean and alert to imperfections; in her view, taking refuge in hypocritical cant was weakening. As far as she was concerned, she said, Loughlin and the others adhered to a patriotic faith that had flourished in an earlier, more tranquil time, when the flag could rally Americans to popular causes with apparently attainable ends; for many people, it seemed to Mrs. Russo, the memory of that time had become both a form of safety and an obstacle to facing up to the complexity and danger of modern choices. Having said this, Mrs. Russo fell silent a moment. When she spoke again, a look of anger crossed her face. Fairly wresting the

words out, she said, "I believe Don Loughlin loves this
country as much as I do."

Quietly, John said, "Susan also has power. She's let her
enemies know they can't have things all their own way.
She's let frightened individuals know it's possible to risk
one's neck for words like 'conscience' and 'hypocrisy.'"

It wasn't until January of 1972, when Mrs. Russo was
still in graduate school, that Judge Burke handed down
his decision. He acquitted the defendants, rejecting, in
his words, the plaintiff's claim that she had not seen a
three-by-five card that Loughlin had had posted on a
bulletin board at the outset of the school year. The card
had included the message, "The Pledge to the flag will
not be recorded on tape this year. All students and staff
members are expected to salute the flag." Agreeing with
the defense position in practically all details, Judge Burke
wrote, "The termination of her probationary appointment
without giving her notice of the charges against her did
not deprive her of due process of law." As might be
expected, Mrs. Russo found the decision crushing.
Apparently, she remarked to me, she needed it to
comprehend that she was in a mean, relentless fight—obvious though that should have been long before the trial.
Rowley moved ahead with an appeal, which would be
filed with the United States Court of Appeals for the
Second Circuit, in New York City, but this time, Mrs.
Russo said, the prospect of a judicial hearing offered no
cheer. She had to summon all the discipline she could to
carry on with her sculpting. Her working conditions were
a balm, she said, for after the decision, I gathered, she
appreciated more than ever the solitude she found in the
school studio. Mrs. Russo told me, "I think busying
myself in the studio made me less of a burden to John. It
hasn't been easy for him." She said that the particular
aspect of Jude Judge Burke's decision that rankled was its
insinuation that she had wanted things both ways—that
is, to enjoy the halo of her conscience while collecting a
paycheck. As Mrs. Russo saw it, her only answer to that

was to demonstrate her sincerity, but then, she demanded, what else had she been doing all along? Didn't it
count that she had persevered in her suit after a year and a
half spent in professional limbo? Didn't it matter that she
had experienced public calumny? Mrs. Russo assumed
that more of the same lay ahead, but she told herself that
for a short while, at least, her deprivations would be
easier to take if she thought of them as a retort to Judge
Burke's insinuation.

In June of 1972, Mrs. Russo received her Master of
Fine Arts degree; she had done brilliantly again, and she
and another student had been honored with an exhibition
of their own work. With that accomplishment behind her,
she went camping with her husband. "That's one of the
important bonds of our marriage," Mrs. Russo told me.
"We disappear for as long as we can. Nobody knows
where we are."

The Russos were away six weeks. They drove West in a
battered Volvo, parking it near a succession of trails that
led to wilderness. Their Irish setter was along, and the
three, each with a knapsack, were gone for days at a time
in remote country without returning to the Volvo. They
wandered through the Rockies, always backpacking,
always moving westward, and eventually reaching
Montana. They travelled light, their home a four-pound
nylon tent. In eastern Colorado, early in their trip, they
hiked seven miles one day and found themselves the lone
worshippers of an immensity that their maps didn't show:
a mountainous recess, circular and deep, its stone walls
forming an amphitheatre of uncommon wild flowers. "It
was impossible to take a step without trampling them,"
Mrs. Russo said. "It was an excitement to be there by
ourselves. When we got back to the car, hundreds of
tourists were milling around the parking area. It put us off
to see them—maybe some, maybe all of them were like
the people we'd left behind." The trip was not a carefree
one. The Russos needed it to clear their heads, far from

the scene of battle; events there had come so thick and fast, Mrs. Russo said, that there had been time only for emergencies. In the presence of the Rockies, she said, they hoped to have a long look at what had happened. Recurrently, in their stocktaking, the two had marvelled that she, in particular, should have done what she had. "Before Sperry, I hadn't ever done what anyone would call a wrong thing," Mrs. Russo told me. She had been reared in what she called the American ethic—working hard, getting good grades, being well liked; she had no political past, at Michigan State or anywhere else. She didn't believe that her refusal to salute the flag represented a belated seizure of rebellion. Rather, she maintained, her gesture was a reaction to issues that had gnawed at her for years: she had thought daily of the war in Indo-China; she had seen instances of racial prejudice, even in the university community in which she had been raised. Her action at Sperry, she felt, was the product of widespread disillusion among her contemporaries.

John Russo said, "It took courage for a conformist like Susan to take her action." Had he been in her position, he told me, he might have organized a protest, might have accepted the help of student activists.

Mrs. Russo shook her head at the idea. "It's not like me to be assertive," she said. "I couldn't ever sway crowds. But apparently I can reject something silently, then dig in." She laughed. "I think there's an element of unpredictability in each of us," she said.

Moving westward, Mrs. Russo continued, she and John often talked of patriotism—the powerful abstraction that had led to her downfall. But, I gathered from John Russo, the grandeur of the scenery through which they were passing also brought the subject to mind—a curious interplay springing up between the topic and the abiding peaks and mesas, the big sky and the iridescent rocks. The more they pondered patriotism, he said, the more elusive it appeared; sometimes it seemed to them that the only way to pin it down was to figure out what it was not. Its

anatomy, however, remained a riddle to them. Mrs. Russo
believed that patriotism was deeply rooted in a feeling for
land. Watching the Western landscape, she recalled, she
and John were more than once tempted to adopt a rustic
existence. It exhilarated her, she told me, that America
encompassed not only metropolises but also the primeval
wilderness that she and John were negotiating. One
freezing midnight, she related, when they were camping
in an alpine meadow eleven thousand feet up, high above
the timberline, a strange event occurred. A windstorm
came up, she said, routing her and John and the setter
from their tent. Suddenly, Mrs. Russo said, their shelter
became the ground they gripped. "We were frightened,"
she told me. "The howling wind brought no rain. All we
saw was a vista of steep cliffs against sharp stars. Our only
sense of safety came from the soil itself. I felt welded to
it."

　　She could never be an expatriate, Mrs. Russo said. Her
"roots" and her "heritage" were American, but she was
fully aware that she was employing words that meant
different things to different people. "Patriotism is a
private matter," she said. She had little use for its
traditional trappings—the bands and the rifle-toting
veterans, the bunting and the speechifying mayors. One
afternoon, she recalled, while trekking within earshot of a
Wyoming waterfall, she fell to wondering what might
possibly persuade her to recite the Pledge. "Nothing,"
she told me, giving the answer that had come to her at
once. Even if America were a model society, she wouldn't
want to pledge allegiance to its flag. In her book, she said,
deeds were of far more use to a nation than swearing
fealty to it. Teaching, for instance. She and John, she told
me, didn't consider themselves well educated. "We
weren't taught to question. We'd like to make up for that
by teaching others to do so," she said. Out West, Mrs.
Russo told me, she came to feel a settled composure
concerning her act of defiance. Perhaps, she said, she
might have behaved differently at Sperry if she and John

had been older and had been parents. But they weren't, and in reflecting on her action from a distance she felt that she had stood up to a special moment in her life. "If I hadn't, I might not be on speaking terms with myself," she told me.

Back in Rochester, Mrs. Russo made an all-out search for a teaching job. Despite a shortage of openings and the publicity attending Judge Burke's decision, she expected to find a place somewhere. "I was believing in a happy ending again," she said. She tried every school district in and around Rochester. Whenever she was asked the reason for her unemployment, she gave a full account of what had happened. On hearing it, one principal said, "I admire your honesty. You're exactly what we're looking for." Mrs. Russo told me, "That was on a Friday. On Monday when I phoned, they said they were hiring someone who had graduated from their school." That was fairly subtle treatment compared with what she encountered elsewhere, Mrs. Russo said. One personnel officer told her she didn't stand a chance at any school—"especially after what those two jerks did at the Olympics"; he was referring to two black athletes at Munich who hadn't stood at attention, in the summer of 1972, while the American flag was being hoisted in celebration of their victory. Another of Mrs. Russo's interviewers stated bluntly that he was opposed to what she had done at Sperry and that he was going to say so to his superior, the man who passed on all applicants. A more amiably disposed official said that he personally would like to engage her but his board would never go along. In another instance, a personnel man checked her application with Sperry; Mrs. Russo wasn't surprised when he reported to her, "You don't have high marks." In all, Mrs. Russo said, she sent off a hundred letters in search of a post, a number of them far beyond the Rochester area. It wasn't as though school openings didn't exist, she told me; for example, a friend of hers, a young woman with

qualifications similar to hers, received two offers in her
first month of looking. As for Mrs. Russo's brand-new
graduate degree, that proved of no value. Indeed, it was
sometimes a handicap. Mrs. Russo learned this when,
after nearly two months of rebuffs and dwindling funds,
she started trying for other types of employment. One of
the first places she approached was Eastman Kodak,
where a junior executive, scanning the educational
background she had entered on her application form, told
her, "You're overqualified for what's open." She reported
frequently to the local offices of the New York State
Employment Service, where interviewers also regarded
her as overqualified for various jobs that came on the
market. One day, a member of the agency's staff, a
sympathetic woman, musing aloud, let Mrs. Russo know
that there was an opening at a small factory that made ink
for printing presses; the factory needed a tester for
purposes of quality control. "I begged her to let me
apply," Mrs. Russo said. But the woman hesitated. The
factory, she told Mrs. Russo, was fetid with chemicals;
the work was arduous; it paid little more than half the
money Mrs. Russo could make as a teacher, and, of
course, it carried negligible benefits. Mrs. Russo, though,
persisted in her entreaties until, finally triumphant, she
proceeded to a dingy plant in an out-of-the-way neighborhood. The instant she set foot inside, she heard a wolf
call; from another direction came the chant "Hire her,
hire her!" Peering into a large room full of unfamiliar
machines, Mrs. Russo saw that no women worked there
but that a dozen men did—all of them, she was to learn,
poorly educated. The manager hired her on the spot; it
would be a pleasure, he said, to have a nice, well-spoken
girl on the premises, what with all the oddballs he came
up against. "He gave me a blue smock," Mrs. Russo told
me. "Any port in a storm."

John hated the factory. Its chemicals gave his wife eye
infections; and its ink, a deep blue, encrusted itself in her
fingernails. "Show them," he said, but Mrs. Russo slowly
closed her hands.

The Appeals Court handed down its verdict in November of 1972, its three judges unanimously reversing the decision of Judge Burke. The opinion, written by Judge Irving R. Kaufman, held Judge Burke's findings to be "cryptic" and his conclusions to be "unaccompanied by any opinion." The appellate judges declared that "Mrs. Russo's dismissal resulted directly from her refusal to engage in the school's daily flag ceremonies," and they described all else as "trimmings." The court did not share Mrs. Russo's views concerning the Pledge, but it did commend her for providing her students "with a second, but quiet, side of the not altogether new flag-salute debate: one teacher led the class in recitation of the Pledge, the other remained standing in respectful silence." Straying from the purely legalistic, the judges said, "Patriotism . . . should not be the object of derision. But patriotism that is forced is a false patriotism. . . . We ought not impugn the loyalty of a citizen—especially one whose convictions appear to be as genuine and conscientious as Mrs. Russo's—merely for refusing to pledge allegiance, any more than we ought necessarily to praise the loyalty of a citizen who without conviction or meaning . . . recites the pledge by rote each morning." Mrs. Russo told me that one passage, in particular, reached her: "Beliefs . . . when they involve not easily articulated intuitions concerning religion, nation, flag, liberty, and justice, are most at home in a realm of privacy, and are happiest in that safe and secluded harbour of the mind that protects our innermost thoughts."

The court's decision brought Mrs. Russo no job offers. It did, however, bring other things, some of them gratifying. Certainly, she said, news of her legal victory came as a relief to her family, in the Midwest. A few friendly letters arrived from strangers, one of them a woman in New Mexico, who wrote, "I hope your action will cause many people to do some serious thinking." The New York *Times* published an editorial endorsing the Appeals Court decision, but Mrs. Russo found it more warming to read a letter that appeared in the Rochester *Democrat & Chronicle*. It came from a former student of hers, who wrote:

> People may disagree with Mrs. Russo's actions; I may disagree. She was, however, a creative, innovative woman who devoted more than her share of time to her students, and to making her classes exciting, different, and interesting. As a student, I felt that the real issue that affected me was the quality of my education, and had nothing to do with the pledge. Mrs. Russo was top quality. What a great loss to the Sperry High School students who never got the benefit of her teaching.

In the main, though, the repercussions of the Appeals Court ruling were on the negative side. The local press dismissed the new decision as an uncalled-for aberration. Letters poured in to Mrs. Russo denouncing her as a Communist and an atheist; one writer recommended an asylum as her proper habitat. Another identified her as a sister of Anthony J. Russo, a co-defendant in the Pentagon Papers trial. She is of English background, but, because of her married name, she was often thought to be Italian. An anonymous correspondent wrote, "Il Duce made us youngsters sing 'Giovinezza.' Why don't you go to Russia and sing the 'Internationale'?" An elderly Italian woman phoned twice to say that America had been good to Italians, and that Mrs. Russo owed it to her people to mend her ways. The phone often rang late at night, no one at the other end. One night, though, someone was: a man threatening Mrs. Russo. John Russo, who answered, didn't tell her about it for a week. At the ink factory, the manager was upset to learn from the newspapers that he hadn't hired such a nice girl after all. "He felt sorry for himself," Mrs. Russo told me. "He said he just couldn't get away from weird types. But I consoled him. I made him a solemn promise that the minute I had a teacher's job I'd leave." Still, nothing could dampen Mrs. Russo's spirits when she heard the decision. "It was a wonderful day," she said. "I found it incredible that an ordinary person like me could win. It proved that the system still had life."

"Ordinary!" John exclaimed. "You had Rowley's organization and its money behind you. Without them, you'd have got nowhere."

But their argument wasn't resolved—at least, not at the time of my visit, for just days before my arrival, as I knew, the Sperry school board had moved to appeal the case to the United States Supreme Court. When John reminded his wife of this, she lapsed into silence, retreating from further discussion.

Before I left Rochester, I tried to find out why Sperry was pressing the litigation. I saw Robert H. Wendt, the school board's lawyer. Receiving me in his law offices, Wendt, a courtly man of about seventy, called it "an unpleasant duty" to take the Russo case to the Supreme Court. He said that the board's decisions throughout the case had been inspired less by strictly legal considerations than by "a conflict of personal philosophies." If it was this conflict I was curious about, he said, I would probably do better to talk to others, for he himself was primarily a technician. This didn't mean, he added, that he was unable to find merit in taking the case to the Supreme Court. He spoke of the power struggle between educational supervisors and teachers everywhere, and then said, "If Mrs. Russo is reinstated, will she have tenure? Has she earned a job for life by her disobedience? If she does get her job back, how will she be received by our public? Should the members of our board be personally liable for damages, as Mrs. Russo's lawyer is asking? If Rowley has his way, how will we ever get board members again? They aren't paid a cent for the long, thankless hours they put in." Sighing, Wendt concluded, "Protest, protest. It isn't so long ago that all that school lawyers had on their minds was bond issues and acquiring realty."

Taking Wendt's advice, I interviewed those whose
personal philosophies had led them to oust Mrs. Russo.
One of them was James R. Breese, a credit manager, who,
as a board member, had testified against Mrs. Russo
before Judge Burke. Breese, who was no longer on the
board, had gone on to achieve political prominence as a
member of the Monroe County Legislature; it was just
outside its chamber that we met. A fortyish, energetic
man of sustained affability, Breese said that, in retrospect,
he didn't regret his opposition to the new teacher one bit.
"She was an insubordinate employee. I was acting for my
constituency," he said. He assigned an almost hallowed
quality to the Pledge, comparing it to a chapel reading.
Breese told me, "The Pledge is a moment of meditation.
You hope that during it someone will think where we are
and where we are headed." Breese wasn't surprised that
the litigation was taking years. At the time he voted to
have Mrs. Russo fired, he had suspected that it might. "I
knew in my gut it wasn't the end of the case," he said. "I
knew it wasn't being resolved with finality for all
people."

Randle Cartwright, who had been president of the
board at the time of Mrs. Russo's dismissal, drove into
Rochester from his suburban home to see me in my hotel
room. Like Breese, he had appeared as a defense witness.
A slender man of gentle mien, he was a retired engineer, a
veteran of long service with Eastman Kodak. Cartwright
regarded Mrs. Russo's discharge as nothing more than "a
personnel situation," adding, "If I thought to tell my boss
where to get off, I'd figure to be looking for a job." He
took no stock in Mrs. Russo's talk of "hypocrisy."
Refusing to recite the Pledge, he said, could result only in
tearing the country apart, but he cautioned me that I was
not to infer from this remark that he had no fault to find
with the government. He told me, "I lost my son in
Vietnam in 1967. He was a first lieutenant in the
Marines." Having said this, he seemed to forget about

Sperry, and for the next few minutes I listened to the politics of a bereaved father—an unbridled attack on American policies, the intensity of which Mrs. Russo or anyone else would have been hard pressed to match. When it was over, Cartwright said, "Why can't things be done the way they were when I was a boy? Sad to say, they're not being improved on."

I telephoned Loughlin for an interview, and he said, "I don't want to discuss the case. That's my judgment. O.K.?" He answered affirmatively, though, when I asked if I could visit Sperry the following day to hear some of its students recite the Pledge. Before I did that, however, I had an early-morning talk with Ten Haken at his home, a two-story Colonial house not far from Sperry. He had made time for me at once when I requested an interview, though he had assumed considerable responsibilities as District Superintendent of Schools for parts of two counties—a higher post than the one he held during Mrs. Russo's year at Sperry. A husky blond man, with an air of careful poise, Ten Haken said that Judge Kaufman's opinion betrayed a serious misconception of the case in its very first sentence: "Events that occur in small towns sometimes have a way of raising large constitutional questions." Henrietta, Ten Haken declared, could hardly be thought of as being out in the boondocks. Sleuthlike, the educator asked, "Did a mind-set take place in which a judge pictured a small town that was engaging in a witch hunt?" Answering his own question, Ten Haken assured me that nothing could be further from the truth. Given the Appeals Court's misconception, however, he continued, it was no wonder that its three judges had stressed the Pledge while scanting what he regarded as "the basic issue." Ten Haken told me, "That issue was not to fire but to choose not to rehire. The issue was to provide best-quality teachers whose relations with their peers, students, and the community would enable them to fit into a total context." Getting around to the Pledge, Ten

Haken said that he assumed I was aware that its recitation
was required by law. When I mentioned that the public
school at which John Russo taught didn't observe the
ceremony, Ten Haken, after a momentary pause, said,
"All I can say is that some people choose not to comply
with the law. I myself find it appropriate to maintain ties
with our traditions. The Pledge is a way of expressing
allegiance to something bigger than ourselves."

Hospitably, Ten Haken drove me to Sperry on learning
that I was going there to hear the Pledge. En route, he
frowned when I voiced my regret that Loughlin had
declined to see me. At the school, he made a point of
introducing me to Loughlin, whereupon the principal,
changing his mind, informed me that we could have a talk
after all. Before we did, one of Loughlin's assistants, a
genial middle-aged man by the name of George Rittenhouse, led me to a classroom to hear the Pledge. As we
walked along a broad, clean corridor, he told me that the
system of Pledge-taking had changed since Mrs. Russo's
day. The Pledge was no longer piped throughout the
school, he said; instead, homeroom teachers themselves
now administered it. Rittenhouse liked the new setup; it
saved him a chore, he said, since he was the man who had
previously done most of the broadcasting. "I was no
Walter Cronkite on that intercom," he told me.

Student traffic was all around us, moving every which
way to homerooms. The corridor seemed charged with
sex. Wherever one looked, healthy, exuberant teen-agers
were in frank flirtation; here and there they were in
fleeting embrace. Rittenhouse and I entered a homeroom
a minute or two before its daily ritual got under way. The
Pledge was over almost as soon as it began, the boys and
girls facing a flag stationed in a corner of their room. I had
no sense of being witness to a meditative occasion, as
Breese saw it. A few students didn't even say the words,
and scarcely for ideological reasons. One boy spent the
time wrestling himself out of his sweater; another tossed
a pencil into the air a few times; a boy and a girl gazed at
each other, not at the flag. But the Pledge did go forward,

its familiar contents audible, the young Americans on
their feet, their posture not overslack. As we returned to
the corridor, Rittenhouse remarked, with satisfaction,
"Seventy-eight homerooms, seventy-eight flags." I followed him to the faculty cafeteria, where I was to await
Loughlin, and, passing through the corridor again, I
thought back on the ceremony I had just watched.
Inevitably, perhaps, I felt a letdown, for, searching the
students' faces, I had had no way of knowing what each
one of them, privately, inwardly, was bringing to the
ceremony; it was impossible to determine whether its
observance was worth the dislocation of Mrs. Russo's life,
the assemblies of outraged townspeople, the time that had
gone into coping with the teacher's unconventionality. In
the faculty cafeteria, over coffee, I asked Rittenhouse
what he thought about saluting the flag. "What's the
harm?" he replied.

He departed when Loughlin arrived. The principal
came in a hurry and left in one, explaining that I had
caught him on an especially crowded day. He didn't have
Ten Haken's style. In his early forties, bespectacled, his
mouth grimly set, Loughlin was a plainspoken man with
an embattled air. His position on the Pledge was more
stringent than his assistant's. He said, "I don't want my
child in a class where the teacher isn't reciting the Pledge.
That's my personal outlook. O.K.?" Injecting Mrs.
Russo's name into the conversation, I informed him of
her inability to find teaching employment. Things might
have been different, he said, if she had followed his
counsel three years ago. "If she had resigned, she'd be
working somewhere now," he said. It was the one point
he made in the few minutes we were together—that Mrs.
Russo had blundered tactically. If she had let him know
her feelings about the Pledge, he went on, he might have
relieved her of homeroom duty. Loughlin said, "I'm not
saying that I would have decided differently, but if she
had come to me and told me how she felt I might have
had a chance to think about it. Why couldn't she do things
quietly?"

I said goodbye to Mrs. Russo in a studio she had rented
in September of 1972, immediately after becoming
an ink tester. The studio was in a decaying industrial
area of Rochester, on the fourth floor of an old building tenanted mostly by small firms. John took me
there. We found Mrs. Russo in a small, high-ceilinged
room that had a sink in one corner; a window opened on a
fire escape. The studio was cluttered with the parapher-
nalia of her art—velveteen, plastics, cotton batting, a
hot-glue gun. Mrs. Russo herself was at a sewing machine
joining oddly shaped pieces of fabric for a work in
progress. Standing side by side, her husband and I
towered over her. Hunched over her machine below the
high ceiling, she looked smaller than usual and, I
imagined, as alone as she would ever care to be. Mrs.
Russo thanked me for coming by, and said that if we met
again she hoped she would be able to tell me that her life
had shaken free of its "holding pattern." She said, "Right
now, there's no planning for the immediate future or for
the future future. It's a good thing John's happy with his
work." She couldn't bear the thought of losing in the
Supreme Court; she wondered whether her case would
dog her after it was legalistically dead. I asked if the past
three years had made a radical of her, and she shook her
head. She almost wished they had; it would be so easy to
rely on pat slogans. But the three years had left her angry.
She blamed herself for having been naive, for not having
mistrusted people enough. Indignantly, she said, "I don't
deserve to be punished. I want to teach."

In mid-April, 1973, the Supreme Court refused to
consider the school board's appeal, and I telephoned Mrs.
Russo to hear what she had to say. She sounded pleased
but wary. Presumably, the new development could
mean her return to Sperry as well as payment of back
wages and damages, she told me, the details of which
had yet to be resolved in court. "The judges and lawyers
aren't done," she said. "I'm still at the ink factory."

POSTSCRIPTS

D_{r.} Spock and Michael Ferber were acquitted on July 11, 1969, when the United States Court of Appeals for the First Circuit reversed their convictions, finding that these verdicts had been based on "insufficient evidence." On a technicality, the same court held that Chaplain Coffin and Mitchell Goodman were liable to retrial, but the government did not pursue their prosecution.

Sansivero was sentenced to a year in the stockade and given a dishonorable discharge. From Father Hayes, I heard tidings of other deserters I had met. Agento became a Swedish citizen in February, 1973. Toler earned his doctorate in philosophy and joined the faculty of a Swedish university. Gershater married and settled in the north of Sweden, teaching English to local workers. The Downeys emigrated to Canada. With the passage of time, political activity on the part of the deserter colony slackened, its members uncertain whether they would accept amnesty were it ever extended.

Christmas of 1972, Frank Reed sent me a card on which he wrote that he had left United Metals and returned to Tennessee, where he was regional sales manager for "a peaceful but profitable plastics company." He wrote, "Lucy and I are living happily in the suburbs of

Knoxville in the higher income neighborhood. We're still concerned about the direction of the country. I'm a Scoutmaster of a Boy Scout troop and am working at a couple of other civic activities. Most of my friends disagree with my social and political opinions, but at least they understand them."

Shortly after the American forces pulled out of Indo-China, I paid a visit to the Pentagon. Not much had changed. I heard the same chafing I had previously heard over the low regard in which Americans held their military. "A victory in 'Nam could have been a shot in the arm," a lieutenant colonel told me. No one openly expressed regret over his country's failure to employ nuclear weapons in Indo-China. The nearest anyone came to that was a civilian ordnance specialist, who told me, "Someday, someplace, we'll use a nuke, and that's when we'll find out the kind of option we've been letting go by."

Thanks to an adroit lawyer—a junior officer—Harry Taggart was a civilian six months after his court-martial, with a type of discharge that entitled him to the benefits that attach to an honorable discharge but that would stigmatize him as a sailor whose Navy career had been less than exemplary. He returned to his home town, where he became a dispatcher for a trucking firm and married a high-school classmate; before their wedding, Taggart promised her he would tell no one he had ever been a deserter.

A day before the 1973–74 school year opened—five months after the Supreme Court delivered its ruling—the district board reinstated Mrs. Russo, granting her tenure and making restitution of $20,000 for, among other matters, deprivation of her constitutional rights and damage to her reputation as a teacher. In addition, the salary Mrs. Russo received on resuming her career was that of a teacher with seven years' experience—two years more than would have been the case had she not been dismissed in 1970. Returning to Henrietta, Mrs. Russo was assigned not to the community's high school, where Loughlin was principal, but to its junior high school. The flag salute was a daily fixture there, too, but Mrs. Russo's new regimen included no homeroom duties; as a result, she and the students were secluded from each other while the Pledge was being rendered.